Eyelash Extension Training Manual

Eyelash Extensions Grafted Lashes Training Manual

***Plus false and party eyelash applications.
With step by step instructions.***

Author
Robyna Smith-Keys

Revised
13th June 2011
20th September 2013
31st July 2015

ISBN
978-0-9875065-9-7

Copyright

Copyright Page
~~~~~~~~~~~~~~

Copyright By Robyna Smith-Keys
Published by Robyna Smith-Keys

Naturally all the copywriter laws apply to this book. If you abide by them you will feel good about yourself, if you do not then heaven help you.

Copyright Key points

• Certain material is automatically protected by copyright under Australian law. There is no
Registration of copyright in Australia, and no formal procedures to go through.

• Copyright gives its owner the legal right to take action in certain circumstances if someone else uses their material. Criminal proceedings can be brought.

• In some circumstances, copyright owners can rely on presumptions that they own copyright, rather than having to prove ownership.

• In addition to copyright, both technological protection measures and contractual terms can be used to limit other people's ability to have access to or use copyright material.

Thank you for respecting the hard work of this author.

Table of Contents

TABLE OF CONTENTS

Copyright By Robyna Smith-Keys	ii
Dear Student	1
Required Skills And Knowledge	4
Dear home user,	6
Eye Skin and Anatomy	7
Eye Skin Care & Anatomy	*7*
The basic processes of growth are:	9
Cell division (multiplication)	*9*
Cell differentiation	*10*
The Growth of the Epidermis	*11*
The Anatomy of the Skin Around the Eyes	13
Maintaining Healthy Skin Around the Eyes	18
Conversion Table	19
Eye Treatment	20
My Favorite Mix	20
Train Your Client Brochure.	22

Aromatherapy Skincare	**26**
Making Skin Care	**28**
Cleansers	*28*
Toner	*29*
Eye Makeup Remover	*29*
Moisturizer	*30*
Skin peels	*31*
Night Creams	*32*
My favourite nigh oil is:	*32*
After sun	*33*
Bath Oils	*33*
Masks	*34*
Aromatherapy Eye Exfoliate	**37**
Healthy Eyes	*38*
Do's and Don'ts:	**42**
Do's:	*42*
Aromatherapy Safe Oils	**44**
Don'ts:	*50*
Aromatherapy Contra-indications	**51**
Important Factors	**52**
Pregnancy	*52*
Phototoxicity	*52*
Sensitization	*53*

Client preference	*53*
Preparation For Extensions	**55**
Tray Setup	*55*
Extensions Procedure.	**57**
Eyelash shapes.	**59**
Eyelash Extensions Instructions	**62**
What are Eyelash Extensions?	**64**
How long do lash extensions last?	*65*
How often should I get touch-ups?	*65*
Questions & your answers.	**65**
Can I swim, shower, exercise, or visit a spa while wearing Eyelash Extensions?	*66*
How long will it take to Apply Eyelash Extensions and how is it done?	*67*
What should I do to prepare for the procedure?	*67*
Beauty Slant Position	**80**
Begin Eyelash Grafting Extensions	**88**
The Most Important Steps	**93**
First step	*93*
Second Step	*94*
The Amount of Glue	**95**
This is very bad	*95*
This is good	*95*

This is better	*95*
Third Step	*99*
Eyelash Glue	**102**
Removing Eyelash Extensions	**108**
Test 1 Eyelash Extensions	**116**
Watch Movie Clip On Grafting	*117*
How to submit your exams	**121**
Forms for client	**123**
Test Two,	**127**
Practice Eyelash Extension.	*127*
Practice on False Eyelashes.	*128*
Tray Setup For practice.	*128*
Test Three	**131**
Eyelash Extension Practice with Teacher	*131*
Advertise Your Service.	**133**
Test Four	**134**
Aftercare Instructions	**135**
Test 5	**137**
Aftercare Instructions	*137*
Party Lashes	**138**
What are Party Lashes?	*138*

Bunches of Lashes	*138*
The Glue Irritation	*139*
False Lashes	*140*

Eyelash Education — **143**

Applying Glue to Strip Lashes — **147**

Party Lashes, Verses Grafted Lashes. — **152**

Watch You Tube Video — **153**

Grafted Eyelash Kit — *153*

A Typical Eyelash Extension Kit — **155**

Large kit — *156*

Small kit contains:- — *158*

Certificate Course — **160**

Associations — **161**

On YouTube — **162**

Piercing. — *163*
Navel set up — *163*
Labret / Munroe — *163*
Rollers out of hair — *163*
Roller in hair — *163*
Hair wefts — *163*
Cosmetic tattoo machine — *163*
Pencil in Eye brows — *163*

Other books by this Author   **164**

Healing And Training Manuals   **164**

Dog Care & DIY Organic Medications   *164*

Foolproof Aromatherapy   *164*

The Antique Healer   *165*

I Was Not Ready To Lose My Mother   *165*

Body Piercing Basics   *165*

Anatomy For Body Piercers   *165*

Eyelash Extension Grafted Lashes Training Manual   *165*

Eyebrow Shaping And Tinting To Suit Face Shapes   *166*

Cosmetic Tattoo Permanent Makeup Micro-pigmentation Training Manual   *166*

An Angel For Cosmetic Tattooists   *166*

Hair Extensions Training Manual   *166*

Supernatural Books:-   **166**

Spell Folklore   *166*

Tarot Scrolls 0-22   *166*

Children's Books:-   **167**

Romeo and Juliette Keep Mark Antony   *167*

Mark Antony Marries Lizy and Has Puppies   *167*

Congratulations   **168**

Student

The index is a very helpful place to find what you need to know right now. However I feel it is best to settle back with a cuppa away from the maddening crow, be they clients, staff or your family and read the entire manual first.

The other point I need to make is:- I do try to make sense in the positions of the information but that is not always possible without repeating myself over and over.

When you first read something you may think but that does not make sense or what does she mean by that? That is why even if you do not understand keep reading and make a note of the page of info that confused you. Then come back to that page after you have read the entire book.

Student

DEAR STUDENT

For over fifty years I was working in hairdressing and beauty salons. During this time I have trained many people to apply eyelashes. They were very popular in the 1950 and are still very popular today. Eyelash extensions lift the entire face giving it a more youthful appearance. If you are not good at following written instructions I have included some YouTube video web sites for you to have a look at. It is my recommendation that you try to understand the written words explaining the do's and the do nots as well as watch the videos.

For you to become an expert at eyelash extensions and gain a good reputation as a professional eyelash extension expert, you must understand the basics of eye anatomy.

We cannot cover all you need to know here in this course. Most of you will have already studied skin science and anatomy. However we have supplied you with enough information to tease your appetite for

Student

knowledge. It is imperative to research your new skills.

Watch the videos we have recommended in this manual before you begin and again every few months later. At Beauty School Books Distance Learning Academe we strive to produce experts. The more you learn about your new skill the more professional you will become. The quicker you become a professional the less you will need to charge and the more clients you will gain. Practice many times as per the practice instructions before you begin practicing on humans.

Before you begin eyelash extension it is important to note that, to gain insurance you will be expected to have completed other forms of beauty therapy training.

WRBCS409A Apply knowledge of skin science to beauty therapy treatments which is part of the WRB04 Beauty Training Package.

It is a core unit for the following qualifications:

- WRB40104 Certificate IV in Beauty Therapy

Student

- WRB50104 Diploma of Beauty Therapy

The guide has been designed to help you develop the skills and knowledge required to apply the principles of eyelash grafting to beauty therapy treatments. We expect you have a good knowledge of:

How to apply knowledge of skin science to beauty therapy treatments

1. Apply knowledge of skin disorders to beauty therapy treatments
2. Promote skin health and care

   Without these elements of competency you should not be considering eyelash extensions as a trade.

Identifying how the skin grows and develops as well as changes that affect the skin over time, will help you to develop an understanding of the affects of a range of different beauty therapy treatments and the techniques that are applied in the performance of these treatments.

For example facial treatments for mature skin may make use of products and techniques that are different for a younger skin. Similarly different massage techniques

Student

would probably be used on a more mature skin compared to a younger skin.

REQUIRED SKILLS AND KNOWLEDGE

Required knowledge

The following knowledge must be assessed as part of this unit: relevant health and hygiene regulations relevant occupational health and safety regulations and requirements infection control procedures and the application of universal precautions appearance of common skin types and conditions, including:

- normal, dry, oily or combination

- sensitive

- pigmented

- couperose

- damaged

- mature appearance of contraindications and adverse effects when applying false eyelashes following in regard to make-up services:

- facial shapes and their relationship to the elements and principles of design

- effects of natural and artificial light on cosmetics

Student

- colour design principles

- colour wheel

- primary, secondary, complementary colours, and grey scale

- tonal value, hue and shade cosmetic ingredients in relevant make-up products, particularly in regard to their likely effects on the skin effect of changes created by specific make-up products and colour application techniques workplace skin care and make-up product range effects and benefits of a defined range of workplace skin care and make-up products.

Client care is always your best tool to success. Your clients tell their friends and their friends tell their friends that you are a cut about the rest.

However a client hops around to different salons for treatments and will know the difference between a competent and incompetent, bungling, unskilled therapist.

To learn the skill to work on yourself and family is great but to learn to work on paying clients is a totally different matter.

Student

DEAR HOME USER,

Hi, if you are considering applying eyelash extensions at home you will find the step by step instructions useful. However we suggest you have your first set done by a qualified eyelash technician. Then perhaps have an instruction lesson from your Beauty Therapist on how to do your infill. The only problem you will have is the cost of the fixative (glue) it is very expensive and as you may not be using it very often then it may go off before you get your money's worth. Retail it's about $75.AU

There are cheaper versions to be found on the internet however we recommend you check the ingredient list before you purchase the glue. We have devoted a section to glue read that before you buy so you are armed with knowledge.

Most manufacturers suggest keeping in a cool dark cupboard not in the refrigerator .

EYE SKIN AND ANATOMY

To become an eyelash grafting / extension therapist you must hold either a certificate in beauty therapy or a diploma.

EYE SKIN CARE & ANATOMY

Our skin is of single and largest organ of our body, not all part of our skin is created with same character. The skin on the scalp has embedded hair follicles; the skin of the nose and cheeks tends to have active glands.

The skin around your eyes is very sensitive and delicate, which needs good care no matter what your age group is. Weather its summer or winter or any other season, follow some simple steps and guidelines as explained below, to have healthier skin around your eyes!

The skin has sweat glands and hairs. As the junction between skin and conjunctiva is approached, the hairs change their character to become eyelashes. Just like hair, the growth of your eyelashes occurs in cycles, which include a growing and a resting phase. At the end of the resting phase, the hair will fall out, meaning that new hair will soon come out. To give you an average estimate of how fast eyelashes grow back, it's anywhere from 1 to 6 weeks. Seldom is each lash on the same cycle, thank heavens. Therefore most people do not notice when the eyelash skin is in the resting cycle. Just like farm land, a smart farmer knows when to rest his paddock and we should rest our eyes from lash extensions.

It is vitally important that the front surface of the eyeball, the cornea, remain moist. This is achieved by the eyelids, which during waking hours sweep the secretions of the lacrimal apparatus and other glands over the surface at regular intervals and which during sleep cover the eyes and prevent evaporation.

The lids have the additional function of preventing injuries from foreign bodies, through the operation of the blink reflex. The lids are essentially folds of tissue covering the front of the orbit and, when the eye is open, leaving an almond-shaped aperture. The points of the almond are called canthi;

Eyelash Extension Training

Now even though the eyes should be moist they should not be weeping in anyway.

The 1st thing an Eyelash technician should do is shine a torch into the client's eyes. If the clients eyes weep or water up do not do the grafting on this client. They may have a weak eye condition.

Growth is the progressive development of a living being or part of an organism from its earliest stage to maturity. Development involves the series of changes by which the individual embryo becomes a mature organism.

THE BASIC PROCESSES OF GROWTH ARE:

CELL DIVISION (MULTIPLICATION)

Cell division occurs throughout a human's life. In any animal, cells are constantly divided to form more cells, either to add new tissue to the existing organism or to replace damaged tissue. This kind of cell division is called mitosis.

CELL DIFFERENTIATION

Cell differentiation is the process by which a general cell type changes to form a cell type with a specialised function.

Although the process for the way that cells achieve this is unknown, it is generally believed that it involves switching mechanisms in the nucleus of the cell. Some pieces of the information contained in the DNA within the nucleus are turned off while others are turned on. Thus, although cell with a nucleus has the same chromosomes and DNA, different cells use different parts of that information just as different students will use different sections of a library.

THE GROWTH OF THE EPIDERMIS

The diagram below shows the different stages in the growth of the epidermis.

1. The layer of stem cells in the germinative layer of the epidermis
2. Cells produced in the germinative layer are pushed towards the surface, become flattened and die.
3. The remains of the cells lose their identity and become converted into layers of keratin. Eventually, these flakes of keratin are lost from the surface of the skin.
4. For better looking skin it is important for us to give these dead cells a helping hand to dissipate. Which is done by exfoliating our skin during the cleansing process.

Dead cells need to be removed every week from our skin to slow down the aging process.

Eyelash Extension Training

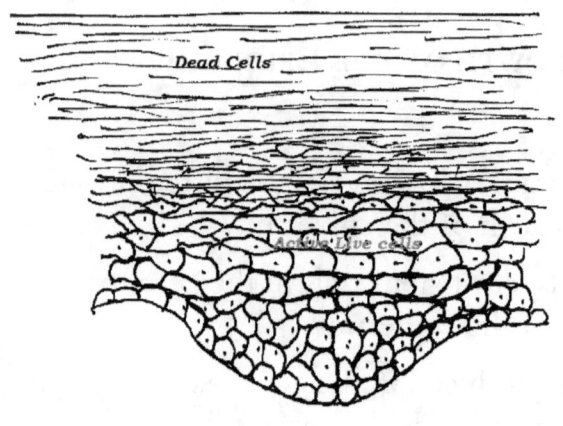

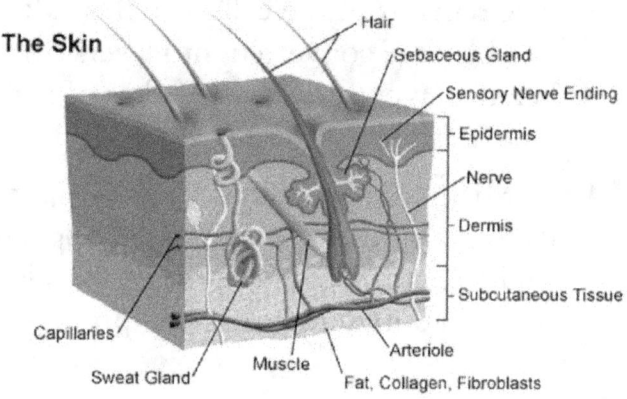

THE ANATOMY OF THE SKIN AROUND THE EYES

Students you do not want to make money at the expense of harm to your client's eyes. Study the skin and lashes. We have supplied you with a brief explanation but you as a caring person you will study the eyes in detail.

The glue you use to graft the lashes can cause eyes to burn. Make sure the client keeps their eyes closed for 10-15 minutes after the procedure so the glue is completely dry before they open their eyes.

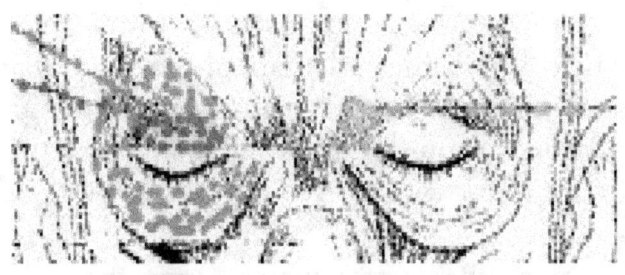

The blue area is he Orbicularis Oculi muscles are circular sphincters which surround the eyes and close the eyelids. They relax when sleeping and can be used independently as when winking. The Pink area is the Levator Palpebrae Superioris muscles sit on the eyelids, open the eyelids and work as an antagonist to the Orbicularis Oculi the green area. The Corrugator Supercilii muscles are located in the orbital arch and draw the eyebrows inwards and downwards causing the vertical lines on the forehead when frowning. Encourage your clients to gently massage this area daily.

The anatomy of the skin around the eyes, also referred to as the adnexa is unique to the face and body. In order to properly care for the skin around the eyes, it is important to understand not only the anatomy of this area, but also the process of skin cell renewal.

Eyelid skin is composed of several layers. The deepest, the subcutaneous layer contains a thin layer of fascia which lies on top of the orbicularis muscle, a muscle that allows the eyelid to move.

Next, the dermis, which forms the support layer of the skin, is made up of threadlike proteins including bundles of elastin and collagen, fibroblasts, nerves and vessels. The top layer, the epidermis, is made up of basal cells, melanocytes, Langerhans cells, keratinocytes and on top, the dead cell layer (also known as the stratum corneum) made up of corneocytes. The epidermal layer gives the skin its appearance, colour, suppleness, texture, and health.

Basal cells reproduce new cells every few days. As these cells migrate upward, they become drier and flatter. Once they reach the surface of the skin, they are no longer alive, and are referred to as corneocytes. This process of migration from basal cell to corneocytes is what gives the epidermis the ability to regenerate itself. This skin renewal process is known as desquamation. Desquamation is an ongoing process that takes about two seeks in a young person, and significantly longer – about 37 days for individuals over 50. The build up of corneocytes gives skin a callous or dry, aged and thickened look. The skin feels and looks rough and its ability to retain water becomes impaired.

There are also clients that have very dry skin around the eyelash area. These clients may have mites in their lashes. Mites cannot be seen by the naked eye. I have submitted two photos for you to have a look at mites in lashes. These photos were taken under a microscope. The only way of knowing if the client has mites is a letter from an eye specialist. If the clients eyes look dry or reddish, explain they have a dry eye condition. They would not be able to have extensions without a clearance letter from an eye specialist. You are not an eye specialist so do not tell them what you think they have.

I have given you this information as a safety tool. You do not want to spread this disease to other clients. This is why the Australia Standards state that a trained Beauty Therapist with skin science knowledge perform the art of eyelash extensions.

Eyelash Extension Training

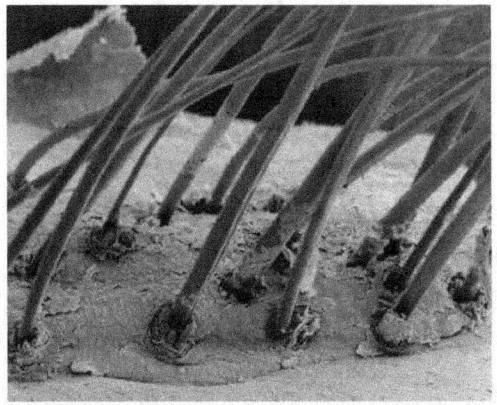

Lash mites on hair follicles – Courtesy of science photo library

Above Photo is of dry skin and lash mites on the hair / lash follicles.

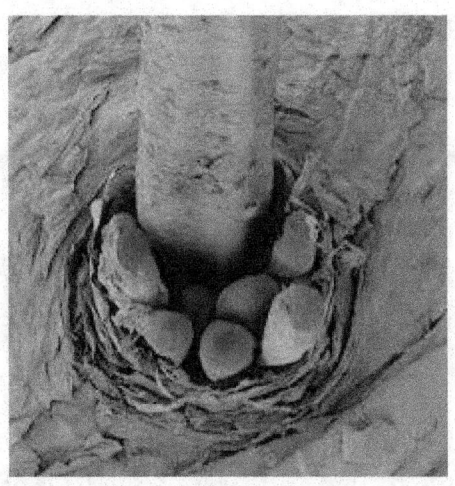

Eyelash mites infestation on eyelash follicle

Eyelash Extension Training

MAINTAINING HEALTHY SKIN AROUND THE EYES

Caring for the skin around the eyes is a delicate process. Because the skin around the eyes is much thinner, it not only tends to be the first place to show signs of aging, but also is more sensitive than the rest of the skin. Therefore, extra care needs to be taken when choosing a skincare product for this area.

Products that contain gentle, non-irritating compounds that reduce the appearance of wrinkles (exfoliates), along with a wide range of vitamins, antioxidants, and skin-plumping substances are ideal choices.

Hence choosing products for the eye area, it is important that it be oil-free. Products containing oil increase the likelihood of clogged glands around the eyes that can lead to stye and other ocular problems.

However an Aromatherapist knows the very best oils to use and prefer oils to creams. Creams are usually loaded with preservatives. Although essential oils are named oils they are actually a liquid.

CONVERSION TABLE

As my books are using our Australian measurements for the skincare recipes I have included this conversions table.

I trust this will assist my readers in other countries. I have also placed this conversion table on the last page of the book for your convenience.

Milliliters	Ounces (U.S.)	Ounces (U.K.)
1.00	0.03	0.04
10.00	0.34	0.35
20.00	0.68	0.70
30.00	1.01	1.06
40.00	1.35	1.41
50.00	1.69	1.76
60.00	2.03	2.11
70.00	2.37	2.46
80.00	2.71	2.82
90.00	3.04	3.17
100.00	3.38	3.52

EYE TREATMENT

My Favorite Mix

In a clean, dark coloured bottle pour 20 ml of cold pressed light Jojoba oil

Add:-
5 drops of Chamomile essential oil
1 drop of Rose Geranium essential oils or Rose oil if you can afford it.

Do not use fragrant oils.

This is one of the most healing and soothing eye oils anyone could ever use on their eyes. This mix would even cure eye mites.

On a freshly cleaned face in the evening just before you go to bed. Pat a few drops on the upper portion of the closed eyelids and just above the cheek bone. The eyes will draw the oils in so be sure not to apply too close to the lashes.

Eyelash Extension Training

Use this mix every night for 1-2 weeks before having the eyelash extensions. If you would like me to mix this oil and send to you please request a PayPal invoice. Email me at beautyschoolbooks@gmail.com

Remember that most eye specialist do not know a great deal about Aromatherapy products. Therefore they give advice on shelf products. Some of the information here is also based on shelf products. All Beauty Therapists should consider taking part in Beauty School Books Aromatherapy Skincare Mixing Course.

Contact lens wearers in particular, should avoid products containing oil. The oil not only sticks to the lens causing blurred vision, but can also cause permanent staining. To minimize the potential for contamination, people should avoid products packaged in a manner that requires "dipping" fingers into a jar.

The above oil should only be applied after removing the contact lenses in the evening.

Eyelash Extension Training

Please refer to this site for more information
www.mediniche.com/ocular**skin**care.html

TRAIN YOUR CLIENT BROCHURE.

In your brochure train your client.

Add some useful information in your eye extension brochure. Personally I love a business card that folds like a card. When you give the client a card with her appointment date you should have a small leaflet on each service you offer and attach it to the card.

~~~~~~~***~~~~~~~

WARNING
Never ever put eye lotions, creams nor oils on the lower lid section near the eyelash roots. The eye has a very strong pulse and will draw oils or creams into the eye. Treatments should be gently patted onto the upper section of the eye lid and slightly above the upper section of the bone structure found below the underside of the eye. So that means the bone around the eye cavity.

Eyelash Extension Training

Starting at the Supraorbital foramen or the supraorbital process bone. Which is positioned about a finger space below the eyebrow. It is a circular bone that also sits above the cheek bone.

Common skin exfoliates are alpha hydroxy acids, often referred to as AHA's. AHA's are a group of naturally occurring substances found in a variety of fruits, sugar cane and milk.

They cause a loosening of the outer dead cell layers, which leads to exfoliation (sloughing of dead skin cells), thereby combating the build-up of corneocytes. The accelerated turnover allows the epidermis to become smoother and softer, and reduces the appearance of fine lines.

By thinning the dead cell layer, AHA's enhance the penetration of other important ingredients. AHA's also act as superb moisturizers due to their hydroscopic (water binding) ability. Only products containing a very mild AHA formula should be used on the delicate periocular area.

Eyelash Extension Training

In addition to AHA's, other ingredients such as moisturizers, antioxidant vitamins and herbal extracts are important for caring for the skin around the eyes.

• Antioxidant Vitamins including Vitamins A, B-complex, C, D and beta-Carotene provide protection against free radical damage. Free radicals are "off balanced" microscopic molecules usually found in groups of thousands. They have the power to do extensive damage to the cell membrane as well as complete destruction to normal cells by robbing them of oxygen. Pollution, UV light, smoking, large quantities of alcohol and daily stress can trigger the production of free radicals. Antioxidants render free radicals harmless before they damage the skin's healthy cells.

• Moisturizers such as sodium hyaluronate help reduce fine lines caused by dehydration. Sodium hyaluronate is the most effective humectant available, and has the ability to bind moisture in the amount of one thousand times its molecular weight.

• Herbal Extracts and Liposomes including chamomile, cornflower, bisabolol and lecithin decrease redness, puffiness and act to nourish, revitalize and rejuvenate the skin.

Notes

Note 1. A vitamin capsule cut open and patted onto the skin gives fabulous results.

Note 2. Cosmetic needling done by a Cosmetic tattooist will repair fine lines even deep lines will become barely noticeably. However you will have unsightly red lines for about 6-12 days.

Note 3. A galvanic facial every week will lift the muscles in your face. You cannot give yourself a galvanic facial so you will need to barter for a good price with your beauty therapist. You should not have galvanic facials until the face starts to drop around the age of thirty.

AROMATHERAPY SKINCARE

It has not been my intension in this book to explain skincare nor to explain Aromatherapy.

Most of you would have done a module or two on Aromatherapy in beauty school while studying for you Certificate or Diploma in Beauty.

Ignorance is bliss but very dangerous when you step out of your comfort zone and into the world of the beauty business.

The more you learn the more you realize you do not know and should know. A Doctor would have studied skin during his/her training to become a GP but they do not profess to know and understand skin complaints. They give you a referral to a skin specialist. However if it is a mild skin condition they will more than likely give you a prescription as a trial to see if the complaint subsides.

Eyelash Extension Training

As an eyelash technician I feel you should at least understand that not everyone can afford to buy top shelf cosmetics. Therefore you should be able to mix some product for those people.

Some of your clients wanting eyelash extensions have skin care issues and those should always be addressed.

Let say they want eyelash extensions but clearly have poorly cared for skin. It is your job to assist them in the preparation for the lashes.

When the eyelashes are extended their entire face becomes more open, with a lifted, younger, more youthful appearance. If their skin, is noticeably dry or dull that will be more noticeable as well.

The Aromatherapy skincare mixing instructions below, although very basic instructs they have been designed for the novice mixer and are very safe product even for a home user to mix.

MAKING SKIN CARE

I have added a very small section on skincare mixing in this book. I feel that everyone will be well advised to mix their own skincare. I have produced other books on skincare mixing. However this section will assist you to get started.

CLEANSERS

First check on what essential oils are safe for you to use. You may as well make a cleanser that is a cleanser as well as a healing agent.

Place 95 ml of olive oil into a 100 ml dark coloured narrow neck bottle.

You can use the bottle the cold pressed Olive oil comes in as it is usually a dark bottle. If you choose to use cooking oil that is fine as all olive oil is cold pressed and safe to use in cosmetic mixing. However the bottle will probably be clear therefore you will need to keep it in a brown paper bag.

Eyelash Extension Training

Add 5-10 drops of your chosen essential oils.

Shake and you're done. Always return the lid to the bottles as soon as possible.

Store in a cool dark cupboard.

TONER

In a 100ml dark coloured narrow neck bottle place 95ml of cooled boiled water. Add 5ml witch hazel
3 drops of essential oil.

The essential oils I use are 2 drops Rose Geranium and one drop of Lemon

EYE MAKEUP REMOVER

Eye makeup remover for stubborn eye makeup.

Place in a small plastic bottle some baby oil and 3 drops of chamomile essential oil. With your finger tips smooth gently a small few drops onto a closed eye. Do one eye at a time. Then rinse/ sponge off with a warm wet face cloth or sponge. Pat the skin dry and wipe over with cotton wool soaked in toner or a very mild astringent. Baby oil is not a healing oil it is a skin barrier.

MOISTURIZER

Moisturizers are simple to make. Use a mix of base oils and 3 drops of essential oils. Pat onto skin 20 minutes before applying Makeup. Also tone the skin before applying the moisturizer and again before applying makeup. A time lag between applying moisturizer and makeup should be approximately 20 minutes. Good time management is to cleanse the face then moisturize. Go and do something else like make you bed or get dressed and have breakfast then apply your makeup.

Moisturizers take time to penetrate.

All too often clients complain that they had their makeup done professionally for a special occasion and it did not last. They also say that the makeup seeped into their eyes and made their eyes watery. This is often due to the fact that their makeup was applied too soon after the moisturizer was applied. The other reason this can happen is the therapist or makeup artist applied the foundation makeup too close to the eyes. Eyes draw product in towards the eyeball that is why you should keep clear of the eye area. Cheap eyeliners and eye shadows will do the same.

Quality eye liners and eye shadows have been designed to set onto the skin and will not migrate into the eyes.

SKIN PEELS

Skin peels should be done at least once a month and never do them daily. They rid the body and face of dead skin cells. There are two very easy ways to give the skin a mini skin peel.

Rub your after sun body oil all over your body.

Place a capful of the oil into a small dish and add one tablespoon of ground sea salt.

Mix then rub this into your oiled body. Rub in a circular motion, as though you are trying to remove something.

Then have a long shower.

The other easy peel is to go to the beach and do the same as above but use the wet sand as your abrasive.

I usually use coconut oil and sit on the water edge while I rub myself with the sand.

NIGHT CREAMS

Night Creams are far more complicated to mix. However if you buy some coconut oil and add a few drops of Clary-sage and a few drops of Lavender plus Rose oil you will have a night cream far superior to anything in the market place.

MY FAVOURITE NIGH OIL IS:

90 mill of olive oil
10 mill of wheat germ oil
2 drops Rose oil
6 drops Rose Geranium
2 drops Clary Sage

AFTER SUN

The best oil for after sun is 100ml Olive or Jojoba or Almond carrier oil to which you add 30 drops of Lavender and 5 drops of Lemon essential oils. Pour a little into your hand rub both hands together and work into your entire body.

Note this mix is too strong for children and for your face so dilute it with Olive oil for your face and check children's mixing instructions in the section headed "A-Z of ailments" in my Aromatherapy books.

BATH OILS

Bath oils are easy to make and are the easiest way of nourishing the body inside and out. If mixed correctly they will assist with the healing process of all diseases/ailments of the mind, body and soul. Refer to my section headed "A-Z of ailments" in my Aromatherapy books for a more informative list of mixing bath oils.

Mix 50 drops of Essential Oils in a dark glass bottle of 100 ml carrier oil.

Keep in a dark place never put on the window sill.

You can always Google what essentials are best for you. If you have no health conditions then you can use most of the safe oils.

Essential oils have pulse. The odour molecules dance in the air. Incandescent lights can turn them into toxic odours. For this reason have a bath by candle light. Have the window and door closed in the bathroom so you can breathe in the aromatic healing odours.

Masks

A mask is something that draws impurities out of the skin and acts as a tightening agent to assist with the ageing process. It further aids the skin from contamination, infectivity, corruptions and pollution. Pollutions in the air age the skin so a mask is a very important weekly skincare process.

Masks may be made from many products.

Sour cream

or **plain yoghurt** may be applied to the skin and left to dry.

Lay in the body slant position for 10 minutes.

Then rinse/ sponge off with a warm wet face cloth or sponge.

Pat the skin dry and wipe over with cottonwool soaked in toner or an astringent.

Egg White

Separate the white of an egg from the yoke whisk the egg white and apply to the skin.

Lay in the body slant position.

This will dry as stiff as a board so you do not want it to pull your skin in the wrong direction.

Then rinsed/ sponged off with a warm wet face cloth or sponge. Pat the skin dry and wipe over with cotton wool soaked in toner or an astringent.

Eyelash Extension Training

Porridge or wheat biscuits.

Mix a little with a small quantity of warm water and apply to the skin.

Lay in the body slant position. This will dry as stiff as a board so you do not want it to pull your skin in the wrong direction.

Then rinse/ sponge off product from your face with a warm wet face cloth or sponge.

Pat the skin dry and wipe over with cotton wool soaked in toner or an astringent.

Clay,

Clay, Corn flour or fullers earth. Clay is by far the best. At the end of my organic skincare book you will find a page devoted to the use of clay. Fullers earth is not to be used on sensitive skin types and may be purchased at Pharmacies/chemist shops or supermarket.

Clay may be purchased from me or most beauticians these days they like to call themselves Beauty Therapists or Beauty Salon/Clinics.

AROMATHERAPY EYE EXFOLIATE

In 50 ml of Grape seed cold pressed oil
-Place 8 drops of Chamomile
5 drops of Rose oil or 3 drops Rose Geranium.
1 drop of Cary Sage

Store in a clean dark coloured bottle, This must be stored in a cool dark place (not the refrigerator).

Once a week for one week.

Put one teaspoon into a cup and mix with either 1/4 (quarter) teaspoon of corn flour or French white clay.

Gently massage onto the closed eye one eye at a time. Remove by splashing cool water onto the closed eye.

Place wet warm face cloth onto the eye and complete the treatment by splashing cool water onto the eye and pat dry,

Eyelash Extension Training

Repeat the treatment for the other eye.

French white clay used as a mask will also prevent the eyelids from sagging/drooping.

HEALTHY EYES

Tips for Keeping the Skin Around The Eyes Healthy

In addition to choosing the proper skin care product, other things are important in maintaining healthy skin around the eyes:

Eye Drops that I so love that do not sting are "Systane" by Alcon Laboratories Australia Pty Limited Frenchs Forrest in NSW Australia. I use these on my dogs as well they are so gentle.

• Drink plenty of water. Water plays a crucial role maintaining the elasticity of skin. But never more than 8 cups a day or there will be a condition that cases the heart to race and you will faint.

Eyelash Extension Training

- Avoid smoking cigarettes. Nicotine constricts blood vessels in the face and under the eyes. Constricted vessels also make it difficult for nutrients to be absorbed, which leads to a breakdown of collagen.

- Stay out of the sun. Overexposure to ultraviolet rays causes melanocytes, the pigment-producing cells, to mature abnormally. This results in age spots and uneven pigmentation. UV rays are responsible for up to 90% of aging and can add several years to your appearance.

- Wear sunglasses to avoid squinting.

- Get plenty of rest. Fatigue can cause skin to look pale and gaunt.

- Limit alcohol intake. Excessive drinking can cause dehydration, so limit yourself to a glass or two of wine every week

- Use cotton balls and olive oil when removing makeup to avoid unnecessary tugging on the delicate eyelid tissue. Olive oil is a great eye makeup remover so long as you completely remove with a hot compress.

Eyelash Extension Training

- Use a quality professionally recommended skin care product for the area around the eyes. Preferable one that is made, by a local Aromatherapist.

By following the above information and choosing a skin care product with the right combination of ingredients will help keep the skin around your eyes looking younger.

To reduce the dark circles around your eyes, no matter at what age you are, you must have at least six to eight hours sleep every night. Sleeping with your shoulders slightly elevated and head tilted towards the mattress would help you working against gravity; which causes fluid to collect in your lower eyelids resulting in dark circles.

Use an eye cream around the eyes to keep moisture in the skin. Better still, use the above eye moisturizer I have given you the recipe for.

When applying cream or make up around the eyes use the ring finger (as it exerts less pressure). Never ever on the actual eye lid. Remember the eye cavity bone is your guide to where the cosmetics end.

Eyelash Extension Training

Don't rub eyes frequently as this can cause an eye infection and in turn causing infection in the skin around eyes. This is because; few of us bother to wash our hands before touching our eyes.

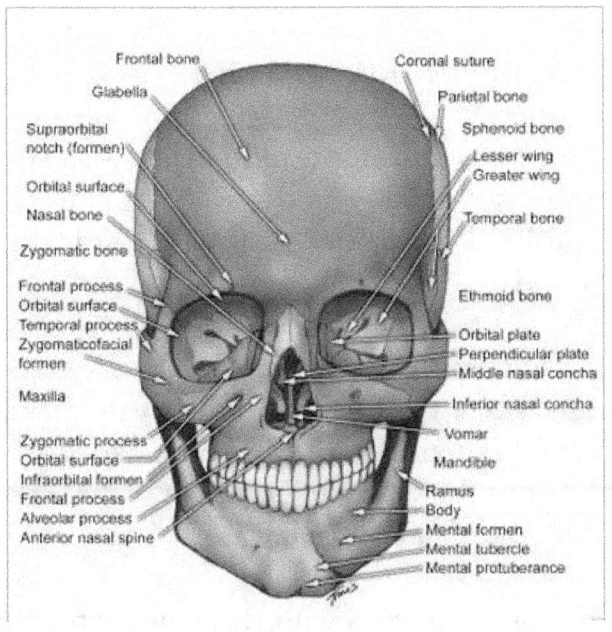

Photo Courtesy of Medscape
www.emedicine.medscape.com

DO'S AND DON'TS:

Do's:

Dip cotton-wool pads in chilled water or milk, lay in the beauty slant position and place on closed eyes for 10 minutes.

A beauty Slant position means you lay down with a pillow under your shoulders. Your head must be tilted back towards the ground.

My favorite eye pad is Chamomile tea bags. Place two tea bags in hot water, take straight out and drain. When almost cool press out the water and place on your eyes for 10 minutes and please relax.

Rinse your eyes with warm water pat dry and apply eye oil not a cream to the upper lid.

If a client complains that their eyes are tired after working all day with computers?.

Then grate a potato with its peel and apply on their closed eyelids for about 20 minutes

Eyelash Extension Training

they must relax completely. This is to prepare their eyes to have firm muscles. Then apply the chamomile tea bags to their eyes.

Sliced cucumber placed over your eyes will avoid developing dark circles.

Give a massage to the eyes, with your little finger by gentle finger movement

If their eyes are red or feeling itchy, massage their scalp with curd, to reduce the unwanted temperature around your eye skin. Also placing and ice pack wrapped in tissues works great.

Whenever possible they should wash their eyes with cold water. This will bring a sparkling feeling to your eye skin.

To reduce puffy eyes. Put two tablespoons in the freezer leave them in the freezer all the time. Each night apply the underside of the spoon to your eyes. Hold on your eyes for 5 minutes.

Always use cold pressed oils when mixing skin care. Always add essential oils to the cold pressed oils, not fragrant oils.

AROMATHERAPY SAFE OILS

CYPRESS - Cypressus Sempervirens
Very popular with men, an excellent deodorant reduces both sweating & odour plus fluid retention.

EUCALYPTUS - Eucalyptus Globulus
Need I explain this Australian oil? The aborigines believed the heat goes into the fire when they burn the leaves and the sickness goes out of the man/woman. It's a cure all.

FRANKINCENSE - Boswellia Carterii
A comforting resin. Used throughout the ages for ceremonies and ritual. Heals scar tissue, but can stupefy the brain in high does or when used too often.

GARLIC - Allium Sativum
Antibiotic, also good oil for the heart and circulation.

GERANIUM - Pelargonium Graveoleus
Anti-depressant, uplifting, great for gall bladder, liver problems acne, broken capillaries.

GINGER - Zingiber Officinale
A body cleanser in childbirth expels the placenta. A digestive aid, great for colic.

GRAPEFRUIT - Citrus Decumana
Uplifting and refreshing. High in vitamin C.

JASMINE - Jasminium grandiflorum
The concrete is mainly used in perfumery, used in China to treat Hepatitis. Aphrodisiac.

JUNIPER - Juniperus Communis **
Mainly used for cystitis and other urinary infections.

LAVENDER (FRENCH) - Lavendula Officinalis

LAVENDER (TASMANIAN) - Lavendula Augustifolia
Burns heal almost instantly. The most popular and versatile essential oil. Relaxing,

comforting and nurturing. Excellent oil for cancer patients. But must not be used for people with low blood pressure.

LEMON - Citrus Limonum
Cooling, it is an excellent astringent for the skin, aids weight loss, arthritis & brittle nails. But may decalcify bones if you or your clients calcium levels are low. Phototoxic.

LEMONGRASS - Cymbopogon Flexuosus
A sedative on the CNS and clears infections. a preservative.

LIME - Citrus Aurantifolia
Used for dyspepsia , colds and fever.

MAY CHANG - Litsea Cubeba
Light and refreshing. A heart tonic for angina.

MANDARIN - Citrus Reticulata

MARJORAM - Majorana Hortensis
Excellent for chest complaints. Non toxic calming.

MELISSA - Melissa Officinalis
Relaxing and relieving. Melissa has a lovely lemon scent fresh, warm & bright.

MYRRH - Commiphora Molmol
Strengthening, a body preserver, great for weak gums ulcers and sores used in 1% dilution.

NEROLI - Citrus Aurantium
Relaxing and soothing cardiac spasm and false angina. Rejuvenates the skin.

ORANGE - Citrum Sinensis
Uplifting. Orange sets the mood for joyful communication.

PALMAROSA - Cymbopagon Martinii
Valuable in skin care preparations because of its soothing and moisturizing properties.

PATCHOULI - Pogosernon Cablin
Grounding. Skin repair, nerve tonic, aphrodisiac.

PETITGRAIN - Petitgrain Bigaradia

For acne, skin toning, widely used in eau-de-cologne.

ROSE OTTO - Rosa Damascena
Nurturing and soothing. Rose is considered the "Queen" of the essential oil kingdom. It is a nurturing tonic for the heart and has excellent benefits for mature and sensitive skin.

ROSE GERANIUM
Similar to Geranium and by far my most favorite oil.

ROSEMARY - Rosmarinus Officinalis
Beneficial for muscle aches and pains.

SANDALWOOD - Santalum Album
Barbers rash, greasy or cracked skin. Encourages peace and acceptance, excellent oil for meditation.

TANGERINE - Citrus Reticulata
Lively, Fresh and vibrant. Beneficial for use in congested, oily and acne skin care conditions.

TEA TREE - Melaleuca Alternifolia
Active against all three infectious organisms: bacteria, fungi, viruses. But please use with

caution. It will also dry the skin out to an unsightly dead look.

THYME - Thymus Serpyllurn Brilliant for muscles and joints, oedema, obesity, sports injuries. Not good for people with heart conditions.

VETIVER - Vetiveria Zizanioides
An excellent moisturizer in skin care preparations, muscles and joints.

The safest oils for skincare when untrained are Rose geranium, Clary sage, Lemon, Eucalyptus and Rose essential oils. I have had amazing results in animals and humans alike with Rose geranium.

A good place to study oils is:-
https://www.organicfacts.net/health-benefits/essential-oils/health-benefits-of-clary-sage-essential-oil.html

Also in my book called the "Antique Healer". If you cannot get my book called the Antique Healer try to find "Foolproof Aromatherapy". It is less expensive and has all the most important factors about mixing essential oils. It is however a much smaller version.

Eyelash Extension Training

DON'TS:

Don't wear contact lenses for extended periods of time or overnight as this makes your eyes feel tiring and hence giving unnecessary strain to your eye skin.

When you splash water do not do this furiously believing doing this will take away tiredness instead wash gently as splashing may hurtle the smallest dust particles or an allergen which may damage the cornea which will again spoil your eye skin as well.

Don't use handkerchiefs to wipe eyes, instead use disposable tissues, which are more hygienic to your sensitive eye skin.

Don't sit near the television a minimum of 15 feet/ 4 meters distance should be maintained from the television and keep your book at least two feet away to strengthen your eye skin muscles.

Use cream based eye makeup as powdery eye shadows can enter eyes and, cause irritation to the eye muscles and skin nearby your eyes.

Do not handle your eyes and eyelids in a harsh manner while using lenses, as the skin will soon loose its strength by handling rough manner.

Don't use your mascara for more than a year, as it may weaken your eye skin.

AROMATHERAPY CONTRA-INDICATIONS

Aromatic plant oils have general precautions associated with them; however each client should be assessed before a blend is recommended.

The following factors are of particular importance when choosing blend ingredients.

A fresh mix made in a salon without preservatives is far more beneficial to your clients' skin than any products you purchase from skincare companies. Oils only last for two year so do not over stock and only buy from large companies that are selling thousands of bottles per day.

IMPORTANT FACTORS

Pregnancy

Certain oils should not be used during pregnancy as they can induce labour. When consulting with a female client you should find out if they are or they could be pregnant. Some clients may find this an intrusive or unusual question to be asked and you should explain why you are asking for this information. Don't assume that certain clients, for example teenagers or older women, could not be pregnant. If there is any doubt it is better to avoid those oils which should not be used during pregnancy. You should also consider your own safety when recommending blends and if you are, or could be, pregnant you should avoid working with those oils which can induce labour.

Phototoxicity

This is an excessive reaction to UV light caused by furanocoumarins (oxygen containing cyclic structures such as bergaptene) which are found in bergamot and the other citrus oils. In a phototoxic reaction the skin absorbs more UV light and produces abnormally dark areas of pigmentation and burning of the surrounding skin. The pigmentation can last for years. When using phototoxic oils care should be taken with dilutions and clients should be advised to avoid exposure to the sun or UV lamps for a period of 12 to 24 hours after product application.

Sensitization

Skin can react to certain oils with an allergic type of rash, blistering or redness. If the offending product is persistently used, contact dermatitis may occur.

Client preference

You should establish if there are any particular aromas that a client doesn't like. If you recommend a blend for its therapeutic properties it will not be beneficial if the client doesn't like the particular aromas.

PEPPERMINT - Mentha Piperita *
Clearing and refreshing a strong, sharp menthol aroma. Not to be used on the face without an Aromatherapist consultation. A small module added to your beauty therapy course does not make you an Aromatherapist.

PINE NEEDLE - Pinups Nigra
Not to be used in Aromatherapy. Gives a great pleasure to a room, wonderful scents and clears away odd smells.

Eyelash Extension Training

PREPARATION FOR EXTENSIONS

Clean all your tools you are going to use in eyelash extension and place them in location easy to rich.

TRAY SETUP

- Cleanser
- Toner
- Eyelash cleaner
- Bowl and towel
- Cotton wool pads
- 2 Good quality rubber sponge to clean around eyes
- Eye Tape
- Protection pads
- Tooth picks
- Premium eyelash 0.15mm or .20mm diameters, of 8 mm /10mm/12mm
- Pad to sit eyelashes on
- Micro buds
- Cotton buds
- Glue black 1 bottle (sensitive) 10 ml,

Eyelash Extension Training

- Glass or jade plate to put glue on
- Glue Remover 1 Volume-up Mascara
- 3 Sets of tweezers curved type to select real lash for extension. Straight type to spread glue on lash. However I use an orange stick for this.
- Mini hand held mirror
- Hand Towel
- Mini scissors
- Rubber air-blower
- 2 sets of false eyelashes. To give client an idea of how their lashes will look.
- Medical adhesive tape
- Pads to protect bottom lashes and skin
- Comb-brush for eyelash
- 1 Eyelash curler
- 2 Eyelash wands
- Paper towel (white)

… Eyelash Extension Training

EXTENSIONS PROCEDURE.

1. Wash your hands.
2. Make sure you have enough light.
3. Check if your customer using contact lens if yes she will to need remove them.
4. Your client must be in comfortable position lying on cosmetic bed.
5. Start out with a clean, fresh face and very clean and dry eyelashes. I'd recommend clean the face with non-oil cleanser.
6. Have a thin and a thick set of eyelashes to show client how her lashes will look. If she has very thick dark lashes show her the thick false lashes. If she has thin natural lashes hold the thin strip of false lashes to her eye.
7. Talk to her about her face shape and suggest the style of the lash shape.
8. **Important:** Do not curl eyelashes before applying extension.
9. The straighter eyelashes are, the easier they will bond with the glue.

Eyelash Extension Training

10. Determine how you are going to place your lashes, choose the sizes of the lashes you going to use and locate near you.
11. Long lashes 10-12 mm on the outside of the lash. Add 8-10 mm in the middle and 8 ml at the eyelid near the nose.
12. Rinse her eyes with the saline mix.
13. Place mild eye drops in her eyes.
14. Check her eyes after asking her to blink several times.
15. Should the client want more lashes you can then begin your second layer.
16. Be sure to place a cold pack on her eyes.
17. Go through the aftercare procedure with her.

The size of extensions will depend on the shape and length the client wants.

Although the clients eyes need a good rinse be sure not to get the glue wet. I usually hold a cloth on her top lashes as I rinse her eyes. Place her head to the side.

Eyelash Extension Training

If you need to remove old lash extensions first see my section on <u>removing eyelash extensions</u>.

EYELASH SHAPES.

It is impossible to cover all you need to know about eyelash thickness and shapes to suit a face type and shape. There is so much to consider. The texture of the clients skin, the colour and tone of their skin, their hair style and colour, their eyebrow shape and colour and an endless amount of other issues.

Until I add more on this subject which I hope to do within the next two years have a read of my book on

"Eyebrow Shaping And Tinting To Suit Face Shapes"

This book is in infancy as I need at least six months to gather photos. Then another twelve months to put the information together. However it will assist you with face shapes.

In the mean time think about this.

Eyelash Extension Training

Almond shaped eyes are very attractive and any eye shape will flutter up quite nicely with lashes that are longer at the outer edge that create an almond shape. Never put very thick lashes on a client with tiny features and fine hair. Never put thin fine lashes on a client that has dark complexion thick hair and thick black natural lashes. Spend at least one hour every night for the next five weeks or so researching before and after shots of eyelash extensions on the internet and start forming opinions.

This is why it pays to have lots of photos to show the client. You will also be well advised to buy packets of false eyelashes of all different thicknesses and volume to hold on one of the clients eyes.

The finale resolution must always be the clients. However you should be educated well enough to advise him/her. A clever adviser always allows the end decision to be that of the one being advised.

When you hold one row of fine false lashes on a client that needs thick lashes you will soon realize that this client needs thick

Eyelash Extension Training

mink lashes. When you hold thick black false lashes on a client of a small build with fine hair and thin eyebrows you will be quick to notice how silly she looks.

For these reasons you need to purchase many sets of false lashes and a variety of extension lashes.

EYELASH EXTENSIONS INSTRUCTIONS

When a client or prospective client makes that first call to enquire about eyelash extensions, do not just quote prices. If you do not have time to explain the different types of lashes ask if you can call her back and what would be the best time. Tell her if you are in the middle of a procedure and what time you will be available for a chat. The client may simply what to book in and that's great.

Take her name, telephone number her email address and make the appointment, no matter how busy you are.

As soon as possible send her an email and a text message to her mobile. You could, while you're on the telephone ask her if she could text these details to your mobile.

However still take her details then ask her to confirm them via text.

Eyelash Extension Training

If she is unsure of the service, you need to talk her through her options and explain the price range and why there is a range of options.

Does the client want a natural look or a dramatic look?

How long does she want to have the lashes for?

Is it just for a special occasion or is it going to be an ongoing look?

You need to explain the different between putting a few bunches of lashes at the outer corner, false lashes for special occasions, the standard 25 grafted lashes to each eye for the natural look and 30 or more lashes for a more dramatic look.

The more informative you are the more professional you will sound.

It is important to send her via text or email her preparation notes. This lets her know all the things she should do before her appointment. All too often you tell them not to wear mascara and they arrive with very thick layers of mascara. That is not her fault it is yours. No one remembers all that they hear and most clients do not study beauty therapy and do not understand the importance of your requests.

WHAT ARE EYELASH EXTENSIONS?

Eyelash Extensions are a popular new service and product that lengthens and thicken your own natural eyelashes. Lash extensions are single strands of synthetic eyelashes that are curved to replicate a natural eyelash. They are applied to each individual natural eyelash one by one for a natural, beautiful and luscious look. Eyelash Extensions are perfect for special occasions or for day to day wear. False lashes are a row of lashes that sit on your natural lashes. They are on a small thin string and are not designed to last as long as grafted lashes. Eyelash extensions have been around since the time of Cleopatra as far as we know. However today's methods are far superior.

How long do lash extensions last?

Properly applied extensions should last as long as your natural lash life cycle, anywhere from 3-8 weeks depending on the individual. Of course rubbing or pulling will make them shed quicker. Aftercare is the key to longevity. An infill every 2-3 weeks is recommended.

How often should I get touch-ups?

We recommend getting a touch up every 2 to 3 weeks. If you wait too long your eyelash extensions will fall out and you will require a full set. Your natural eyelashes fall off every 45 - 60 days due to the natural growth cycle and are naturally replaced with the growth of a new eyelash. Other factors such as exposure to steam or touching your eyes a lot may cause the extensions to fall sooner. A touch up is needed to fill in any lashes that have fallen. Touch ups average about 45 minutes.

QUESTIONS & YOUR ANSWERS.

These are some of the questions I have found clients ask and an idea on how to answer those questions.

CAN I SWIM, SHOWER, EXERCISE, OR VISIT A SPA WHILE WEARING EYELASH EXTENSIONS?

Yes. The bonding agent we use is waterproof and allows you to shower, swim, exercise etc. Special care is required yet overall maintenance is low. We do recommend however that you **do not** wash your eye area for about 3-5 hours after the eyelash application. Try not to cry as tears contain salty liquids. Our new, industry leading eyelash extensions adhesive no longer requires the 12 - 24 hours . We will give you our complete aftercare procedures.

Eyelash Extension Training

HOW LONG WILL IT TAKE TO APPLY EYELASH EXTENSIONS AND HOW IS IT DONE?

The application process for lash extensions normally takes anywhere from 45 min. - 1.5 hours. You will lay comfortably on a massage or facial table with your eyes closed. The Eyelash professional will then apply an under eye gel pad to cover your lower lashes. Then the extensions will be applied to each individual eyelash on a hair by hair basis. Then your infill treatments will take 20 -40 minutes.

WHAT SHOULD I DO TO PREPARE FOR THE PROCEDURE?

1. Please refrain from applying eye makeup prior to coming in for the procedure. The extensions are connected with glue and therefore any debris may shorten the lifecycle of the extensions and cause them to fall off earlier. In the case makeup application is inevitable, we do have makeup remover and face wash available at our salon for your

Eyelash Extension Training

convenience. We also offer a full cleanse service for a small fee of (put a price here).

2. We recommend that you remove your contact lenses prior to receiving the procedure because your eyes will be closed while receiving your eyelash extensions and your contact lens may cause eye dryness. Removing contacts will remarkably increase comfort level. We have a contact lens disposable case here for your contact lens there is a small charge for them or you may bring your case with you. We will email you the prep sheet.

~~~ * ~~~

First be sure to choose the right glue use latex rubber based glue is what most suppliers offer. You need to find glue with no Formaldehyde or Cyano Acrylate. I know that Blinks Advanced glue has Cyano Acrylate in it. Be sure to ask questions about their other types of glue.

Ask client to clean their eyelashes with olive oil one- two days before the procedure and thoroughly remove all dry skin around their eyes. They could use a tiny pinch of ground sea salt mixed with the olive oil. To remove the mix they first use soft tissues. second, with warm face cloth, third with a mild cleansing lotion. This method is very time consummating but more gentle on the delicate eye skin.

You must explain that they should not ever remove the lashes themself with eyelash removing products as they have strong chemicals that may harm their eyes. You have a duty of care to all people at all times.

Ask the client not to wear eye makeup nor mascara one –two days prior to the treatment.

If the clients have not performed the above procedure then please do a complete cleanse of the eye area before you begin. Use a warm compress several times to be sure all cleaning products are completely removed.

Then apply an ice pack for five minutes to close the skin pores.

In their preparation sheet add a small explanation of why it is important not to wear mascara for one to two days prior to treatment. Cleaning the lashes methodically on the same day as the extensions are applied lessens the ability for the glue and their natural lashes to bond.

Lay the client on a comfortable bed that has been lowered so you can sit looking over the top of her eyes before you begin. Her head should be tilted back so you can see their natural lid line.

Never ever have the client sitting in a chair. In a Hairdressing salon you may have them at the shampoo basin with a pillow under their neck, providing you are standing on a step beside them and they are comfortable. You also need to be able to move around the client freely. Also you must be at least 600 mm above their eyes.

I strongly recommend you only do this for false and party lash application. Never have them at the basin for eyelash grafting.

Be sure you have checked with the client as to how long she wants the lashes. Show her some photos of different lengths.

Fill in the client form. However this should be done during the consultation time.

Eyelash Extension Training

It is unwise to trim the lashes after they are complete. The lashes have been manufactured to curve at 3 mm above the base. That is why they come in a range of sizes. The manufacturers have gone to great lengths to tapper the lashes at the tip and if you trim them they will look blunt and unnatural.

Be sure you have checked her face shape and know the correct style and shape of the lashes for the client. Refer to book "Eyebrow Shaping & Tinting" In section covering face shapes.

Place a few lashes on a smooth white makeup sponge.

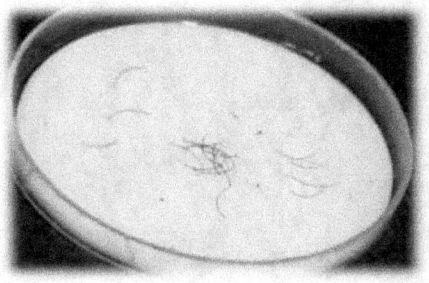

Place the sponge on the bed near her head

Eyelash Extension Training

Or if using the lashes that come in strips have them placed close to the clients head.

Note: This type of lashes come in different ways. I like to buy the strips that have all the different size lashes on the one

strip . I place the strip on either the clients forehead or on the wrist of my **non** dominate hand. Which is my left hand.

Eyelash Extension Training

In the below photo I have I have suggested what size lashes to place. The inner corner use 8 or 9 mm

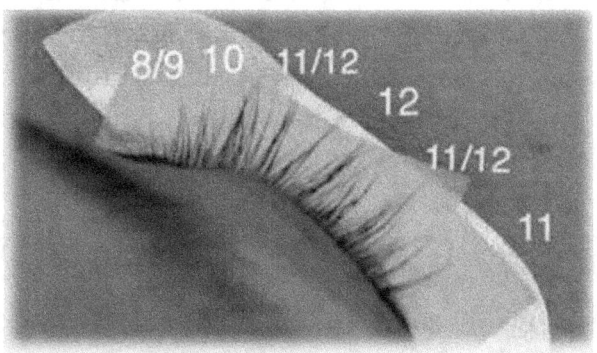

Now clean the eye area with cleaning fluid. Use a cotton pad to apply and dry with clean cotton pads.

Next use the pump to blow the eye lashes dry.

The natural lashes must be completely cleaned and free of residue. Their natural lashes must be soft and exceptionally free of oil.

Eyelash Extension Training

With the clients eyes open place a piece of glad wrap or masking tape under the upper lashes and over the bottom lashes.

Be sure the wrap does not touch their eyeball and that it completely covers the bottom lashes. You are covering the bottom lashes so you can protect them from glue and to prevent the top and bottom lashes sticking together.

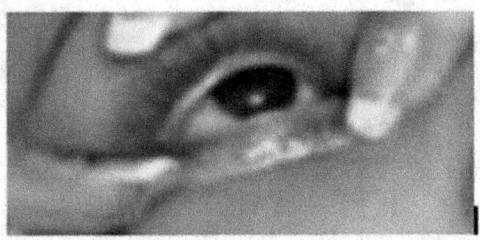

Then brush the upper lashes to be sure the upper lashes are sitting above the glad-wrap and the lower lashes are sitting under the glad wrap.

Put a tiny amount of glue onto a piece of glass.

Place the glass close to the client on the bed or their chest.

Eyelash Extension Training

Ask the client to close their eyes and keep them closed for the entire procedure.

Comb the upper lashes.

I actually do not use cotton pads when apply lashes I use tape or plastic wrap to protect the skin. The cotton pad can stick to the glue. But I used a pad in this photo so you could see me separating the lashes to have just one lash in between my tweezers.

Brush and comb the lashes well.

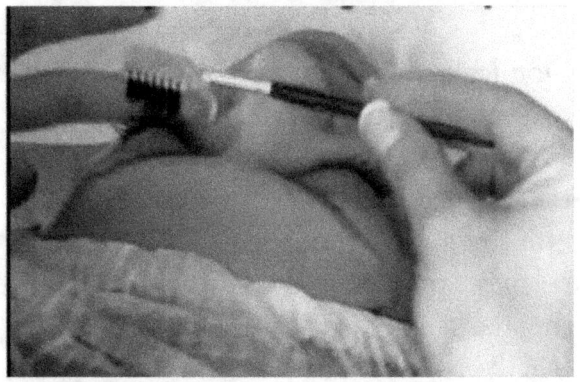

Use your tweezers to push the lashes away from where you are going to apply the lash.

Eyelash Extension Training

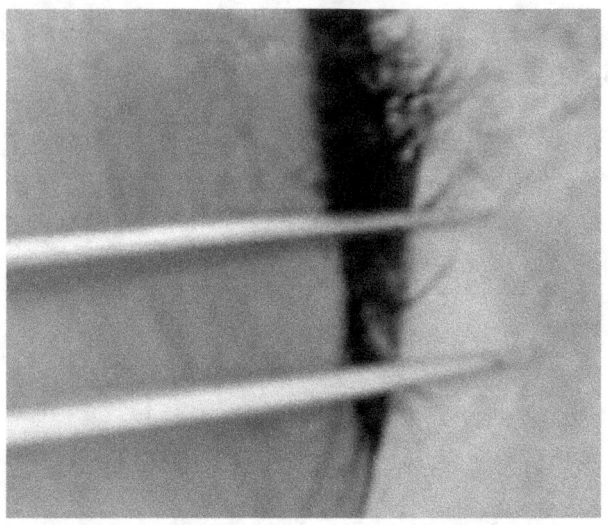

One lash only must be between the open tweezers.

Pick up the thin end of the lash on and dip the thicker end into some glue. Less is best. If you pick up too much glue wipe it off on the glass.

Or on a thick eye pad that you have stuck to under the eyes.

Eyelash Extension Training

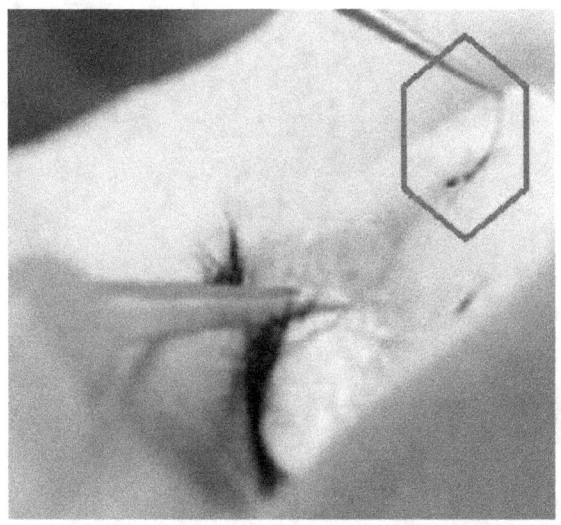

When you have dipped the eyelash in glue, brush the excess glue off the lash extension.

In the above photo the new lash that has been dipped in glue is being wiped before being placed on the natural lash. This decreases the amount of glue that is being put onto the natural lash. Too much glue and the clients will feel like they have heavy eyes.

In the photo above I have drawn a red polygon around the lash that is being wiped before being applied to the natural lash. It is imperative to wipe the excess glue off the lash before applying it to the natural lash.

Eyelash Extension Training

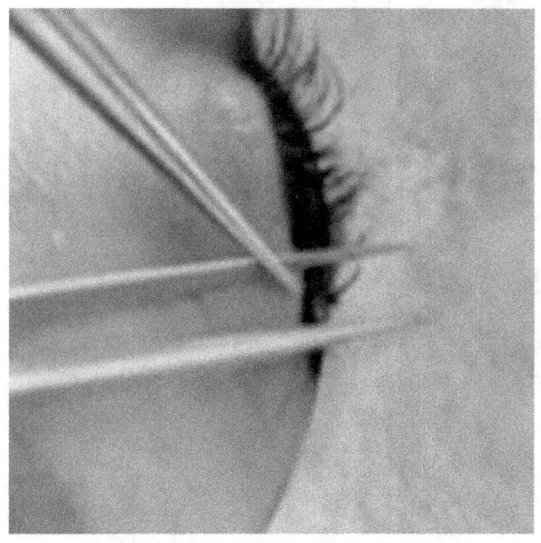

Run the glue that is on the new lash up the length of the clients own lash. This will ensure the new lash sticks to the clients lash the full length of the clients natural lash.

Apply the lash to one of the client's lashes about **1 mm** up the lash. Not at the root but close to the root.

Never ever touch the skin with the glue.

It is important to go from one eye to the other. Put two lashes at the outer corner of each eye. Then two lashes at the inner corner,

Eyelash Extension Training

of each eye. Then put two in the center of each eye.

Keep infilling each eye a few at a time on one eye then a few on the other eye. Never ever complete one eye first.

Repeat this process until you have 25-30 lashes on both eyes. Should the client want more, you will need to charge them for the extra lashes, glue and your time.

When you have completed the lashes use a hand blower to dry the lashes. The clients love this.

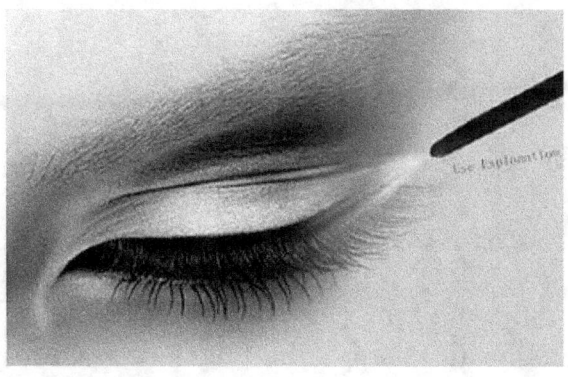

Do not use a hair dryer. The dryer below is also used for drying photos.

Eyelash Extension Training

The air drying photos are compliments of lightinthebox.com

BEAUTY SLANT POSITION

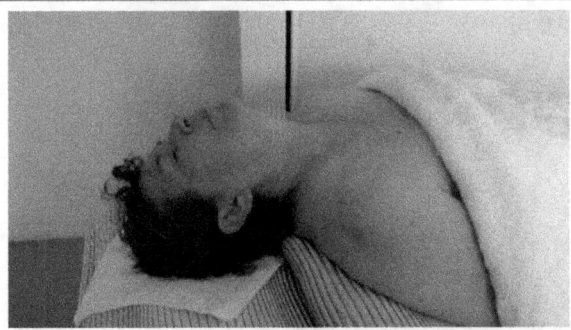

We talk about the beauty slant position throughout all my Beauty School Books. The clients head must be tilted back so the eyes are in line with the shoulders. Place an extra pillow under her shoulders and ask if he/she is comfortable.

Eyelash Extension Training

Now separate all the lashes with your tweezers.

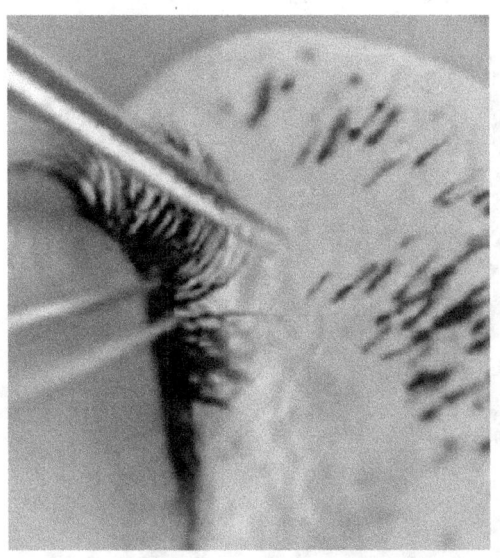

You can also use a tooth pick. I like to use tooth picks to separate the lashes and remove excess glue as I apply each lash.

Therefore I have a packet of tooth picks on my tray.

Then lift the lashes to be certain they have not stuck to the bottom lashes or the pad covering the bottom lashes.

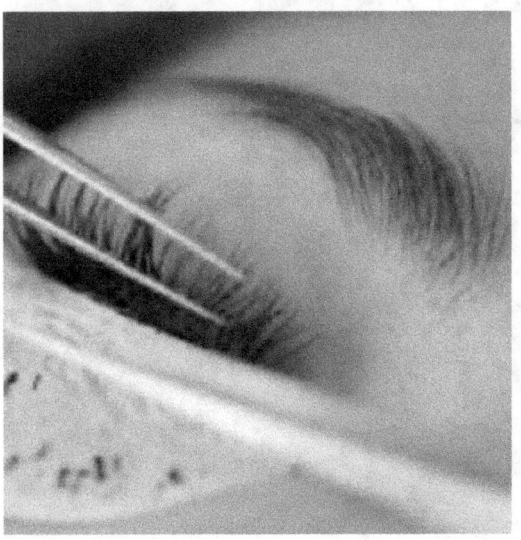

Remember to have the client, move a few times during the process. About every fifteen minutes or so.

Change their pillows and fluff the pillows up again. They can become very sore and stiff from laying there so still for such a long time.

For people with a full face the lash sizes will be longer from the outside and graduate down to 8 mm long lashes on the inner part of the eye near the nose. This type of shaping suits almost all face shapes.

However for an aged face it is often best to make the longer lashes in the middle of each eye.

The best way to determine what suits the client and what is best for them is to hold a set of false lashes on one eye and ask what they think. Then a different shape, false lash on their eye.

The glue can feel brittle after a week or so. Therefore you need to be sure not to put the new lash near the skin and be certain you have very little glue on the lash. So little you cannot actually see the glue.

Believe me. It is so irritating that you will be constantly scratching the roots of your lashes. One time I felt as though I had tiny pieces of steel toughing my eyes. The therapist had put the glue too close to my eyelash roots and she used glue to make the lashes look thicker. I loved the look of my lashes but the irritation was too much to bear. For this reason I had to have the extensions removed a week after they were done. I was not happy as it was Christmas time and I had paid top dollar to look good for the festive season.

Never put more lashes than 30 on each eye. They will be too heavy. After the glue has dried on both eyes show the client.

Should the client want more lashes you can then begin your second layer. However if this is the clients 1st time at having eyelash extensions then suggest she come back in a week time for another layer.

Below in this photo consider the black is the natural lash and the red is the added lash. In this photo all these positions are incorrect.

Eyelash Extension Training

These positions (in red) are all wrong.

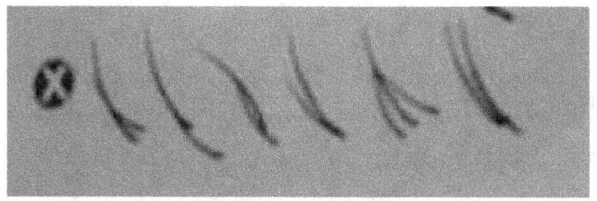

Lets say the black lines are eyelashes and the red lines are the grafted lashes

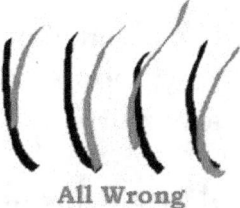

All Wrong

Below under the heading "Begin Eyelash Extensions" is your procedure sheet. Always check your tray set up and your procedure sheet before you begin.

Every salon should have a procedures manual. In that manual under each heading you should have a procedure and tray set up for every service you offer in your salon. If you have staff they should study the manual and be quizzed from time to time on the procedures and tray set ups. You should never expect that they will get all the answers

Eyelash Extension Training

right. After all that is why you have the manual. The manual also helps the single operated salons to always get it right.

The most important fact is: knowing where the information is. When you quiz your staff you should observe who brings the manual to the meeting and who does not.

I would tell my staff we are going to have an open book quiz. I always ran the quiz before work.

How many times in your work day have you forgotten to put something important for the service on your tray?

You are setting up the room and you are called away to answer a clients question or to take a telephone call. We are distracted many times when we are busy and procedure manuals keep us professional.

The quiz time gives you the opportunity to observe those that know how to reference the notes they need in a heartbeat and those that barely have a clue. They are the ones that are not using the manual because they know it all. They are the staff member that all too often makes mistakes.

Eyelash Extension Training

BEGIN EYELASH GRAFTING EXTENSIONS

This is your procedure sheet. Always check your tray set up and your procedure sheet before you begin.

Before you begin set up your work area.

Take a close up photo of the clients' eyes and add to her file.

Fill in the client form.

Check to see what size lashes you should use on the client.

Show her a few photographs of your work.

Hold a set of false lashes on one eye so she can judge the length and thickness.

Lay the client on a comfortable bed.

Never ever have the client sitting in a chair.

Eyelash Extension Training

Be sure you have checked with the client as to how long she wants the lashes.

Place a few lashes on a smooth white makeup sponge.

Place the sponge on the bed near her head

Or if using the lashes that come in strips place them close to the clients head.

Now clean the eye area with cleaning fluid. The lashes must be soft and exceptionally free of oil.

With the clients eyes open place a piece of glad wrap or masking tape under the upper lashes and over the bottom lashes.

Then brush the upper lashes to be sure the upper lashes are sitting above the gladwrap and the lower lashes are sitting under the glad wrap.

Put a tiny amount of glue onto a piece of glass.

Eyelash Extension Training

Place the glass close to the client on the bed or their chest.

Ask the client to close their eyes and keep them closed for the entire procedure.

Comb the upper lashes.

Brush the lashes well.

Use your tweezers to push the lashes away from where you are going to apply the lash.

One lash only must be between the open tweezers.

Pick up the thin end of the lash and dip the thicker end into some glue. Less is best.

When you have dipped the eyelash in glue, brush the excess glue off the lash extension.

Run the glue that is on the new lash up the length of the clients own eyelash.

Apply the lash to one of the client's lashes about **1 mm** up the lash. Not at the root but close to the root.

Eyelash Extension Training

Never ever touch the skin with the glue.

Keep infilling each eye a few at a time on one eye then a few on the other eye. Never ever complete one eye first.

Repeat this process until you have 25-30 lashes on both eyes.

When you have completed the lashes use a hand blower to dry the lashes.

Do not use a hair dryer. The dryer below is also used for drying photos.

Now separate all the lashes with your tweezers.

Then lift the lashes to be certain they have not stuck to the bottom lashes or the pad covering the bottom lashes.

Eyelash Extension Training

Remember to have the client, move a few times during the process. About, every fifteen minutes or so.

Change their pillows and fluff the pillows up again.

Never put more lashes than 30 on each eye. They will be too heavy.

After the glue has dried on both eyes show the client.

Rinse her eyes with the saline mix.

Place mild eye drops in her eyes.

Check her eyes after asking her to blink several times.

Should the client want more lashes you can then begin your second layer.

Be sure to place a cold pack on her eyes.

THE MOST IMPORTANT STEPS

FIRST STEP

The first most important step is the "Correct Position"

Assuming the black line is the natural lash and the red is the graft lash.

First 2 are good
Third is Ok

This position is correct. Place the lash extension onto the natural lash slightly above the root. Also be sure it contours against the natural lash. They should be attached to at least 85% of the natural lash. You can dip the tip into the glue then stroke the natural lash all the way up the lash with the glue that is on the extension. Then position the extension 1-2 mm up from the root.

Remembering not to ever put glue on the root of the lash. You must start 1 to 2 mm above the root.

SECOND STEP

The Second Most Important Steps

Be sure the lash is sitting with the curve the same way as the natural lash curves. Sometimes when you pick the lash up with the tweezers you need to use your fingers to sit the lash in the tweezers the right way.

If you get this step right they will have great lashes that stay on for at least 2 months.

However they will need to have infill's done during that time. The clients own natural eyelashes will fall out and hence the extension will go with it. Then a new lash will grow in the same place. The less glue you use the better.

THE AMOUNT OF GLUE

THIS IS VERY BAD

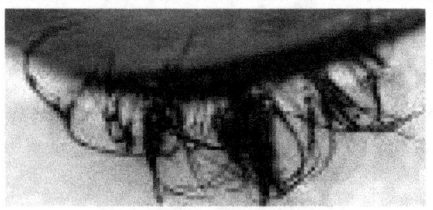

THIS IS GOOD

THIS IS BETTER

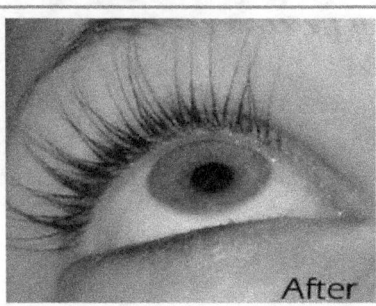

Eyelash Extension Training

There are only a few lashes that have a tiny bit too much glue. The above photo "after" photo is a job well done.

Below in this photo the student has placed too much glue on these extensions. If you look closely she has also put glue onto the skin.

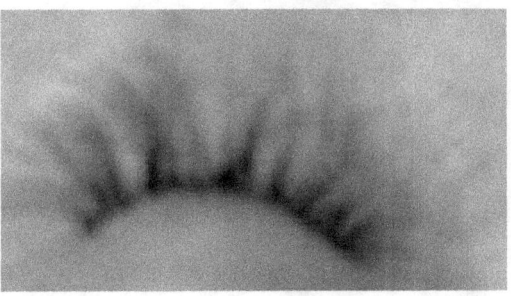

The student put the glue too close to the root. It is very messy.

In the next photo I have outlined the lash with glue on it in a red circle. She did not wipe off the excess glue from the extension lash before applying it to the natural lash.

Eyelash Extension Training

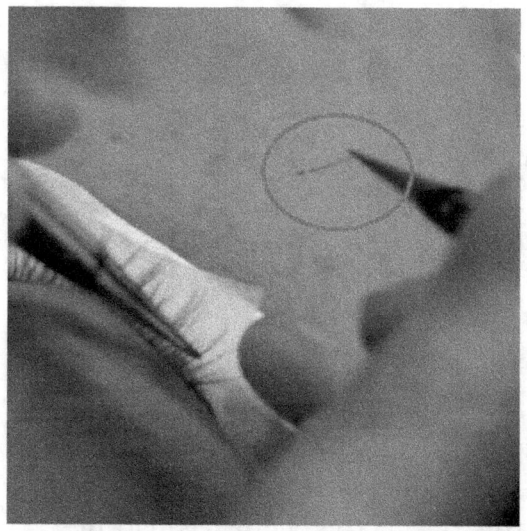

Also she does not have the lashes properly separated.

Watch u-tube videos
http://www.youtube.com/watch?v=DrMdsOvStwI

You will soon get to know which videos are excellent and the ones that are a disgrace to our trade.

Eyelash Extension Training

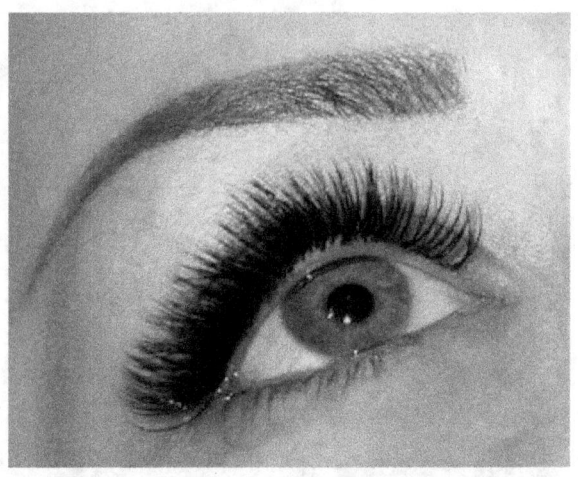

In this photo the client has had her eyebrows cosmetically tattooed. The therapist has tattooed the eyeliner close to the lashes on the outer side of the eye. Then she tattooed the inner part of the eye, inside the eye. That is illegal in Australia and as our standards are recognized internationally I would think it is illegal everywhere.

More to the point for this book; she has applied thick mink lashes and the glue is too close to the eyelash roots. At first glance this looks like a great set of extensions but they have been poorly applied. You can tell that the lovely looking woman eyes are watering in the corner. That because there is glue slightly on the inner lid.

THIRD STEP

The Third Important Step is

"The Amount of Glue" and by far the very most important step. Too much glue causes problems. Get this wrong and the glue will irritate the eye. It could even cause damage to the delicate skin and the eyeball. After a day or two the glue sets so hard it is like fine strips of Steele.

You place a small drop of glue onto a small glass plate.

Pick up the lash in the middle of the lash or the middle of the bunch of lashes. This will depend on whether you are applying single lashes or applying bunches of lashes.

When you dip the thick end of the lash extension into the glue be certain to wipe it on the glass as it needs to be just a tiny amount of glue on the base of the lash.

With eyelash grafting be sure that only one of the clients natural lashes is between the tweezers.

Eyelash Extension Training

With a stroking motion attach the lash as per the video. Be sure the lash sits along the natural lash.

When you attach a couple of lashes use a tooth pick to roll off the excess glue from the underside of the lashes. The toothpick should only be used once and then a new one used on the next few lashes. I actually do this with every bunch I place on the lashes.

For bunches of lashes there is no need to separate the natural lashes. Just sit the bunch onto the natural lashes in the correct shape. By that I mean both the bunch and the natural lash should be in a "J" shape running up towards the eyebrow.

Note some peoples natural lashes have a few lashes that are sun damaged and curl downwards. In this case you will need to curly their lashes with a warm curling wand before you begin.

There are a few different shapes and you will need a supply of all of them.

Eyelash Extension Training

Watch This video on Youtube.

https://www.youtube.com/watch?v=AfWEpUCV_cA

The therapist does a lovely job. She does not dry the lashes with the blower but I feel she has done a perfect job in every other way.

EYELASH GLUE

Cautions:

- Buy glue for professional use only
- Check ingredients list methodically.
- Eyes must remain closed during entire procedure
- Keep out of reach of children
- Avoid contact with skin
- In case of contact with eyes, flush with saline solution for 10 minutes and consult a physician immediately
- Keep in cool and dry place
- Avoid direct sunlight
- Shake well before using

Eyelash Extension Training

Blink Lash Style & Care Glue. They say it is the best on the market today. No sting and dries quickly.

Never ever keep any glue in the refrigerator.

I have not checked the ingredients of this glue. I know that Blinks "Advanced glue" has Cyano Acrylate in it. Therefore I would not use it if I was still working in the industry. They have lots of other glues so check out their ingredients.

As you would know I am now retired therefore, I have not ordered glue for about six years. In 2007 my glue cost me about $125 and is no longer on the market. Eyelash glue has come down in price and has improved considerably. It has been my experience in life that the more people in your industry you associate with the more you feed off each others knowledge. Ask other therapist what they are using and what kind of results they are having with that product. But still check the ingredients list.

Have your eyebrows waxed regularly at other salons. This way you get to meet other beauty therapist and build a rapport or friendship and talk about products. If your supplier is not a therapist they will only be giving you the info they have been feed by the manufacturer.

Ring, Ring Cup and Stone pad. The glue can be placed in a ring or on a stone pad or a small piece of glass.

Some salon eyelash glue contains dangerous chemicals such as Formaldehyde. Other salon suppliers have eyelashes glue or adhesives that contain Cyano Acrylate.

Abstract
From
http://www.ncbi.nlm.nih.gov/pubmed/17388821

Cyanoacrylate (CA) and its homologues have a variety of medical and commercial applications as biological adhesives and sealants. Homologues of CA are being widely promoted in surgery as a tissue adhesive to replace traditional suturing techniques. Potential benefits of using CA adhesives include better cosmetic results, more rapid wound closure, and perhaps most significantly, the potential for significant reductions in percutaneous injuries from suture needles, which would in turn also reduce the risk of transmission of infectious diseases. Nevertheless, certain concerns have been raised regarding the potential toxicity of CA within patients, as well as among health professionals who are occupationally exposed when using CA compounds. Reported toxicity of CA in the workplace may result in dermatological, allergic and respiratory conditions. To help reduce the occupational burden, therefore, medical staff using CA adhesives should avoid direct contact with the compound and use appropriate personal protective measures at all times. Maintaining higher levels of humidity, optimizing room ventilation and using special air conditioning filters in surgical suites and operating theatres may also be useful in minimizing the exposure to volatile CA adhesives.

Eyelash Extension Training

The above a **Abstract** should give you an idea of the type of research you should do about what you are placing on your client and the effects these product have on you and other salon members.

The semi permanent eyelash glue can be hard to remove and eventually clients will pull out their own eyelashes. Try to find special eyelash adhesive that has no Formaldehyde or Cyano Acrylate. However the bond is not as long lasting. I recommend using the stronger glue but if the eyelash glue becomes too brittle then remove with olive oil.

Rub each lash and use fingers to create a friction on the lash and ease off. Then clean the lashes with a warm soap and water mix.

Leave lashes off for a few weeks then start again. I have been having my lashes done for many years and yes sometimes my own lashes come out but I still have plenty not that I ever had great lashes. Most of the lashes do grow back if the therapist stays away from the eyelash root with the glue.

See below for more information on eyelash removal.

Eyelash Extension Training

Did you hear me do not allow the glue to touch the eyelash skin or the eyelash root.

I have found that the most expensive ones are not what they say they are. I have paid one hundred and twenty five dollars for extension glue and it was not as good as the glue I paid seventy five dollars for. They have come down in price over the years. They now sell glue for around forty dollars. Be sure to check the ingredients list. Then Google the names on the list.

If the ingredients are safe it does not matter what the price is.

REMOVING EYELASH EXTENSIONS

How to remove the extensions will depend greatly on how much glue was applied and what type of glue was used.

To remove eyelash extensions is somewhat dangerous. You must protect the clients delicate skin around the eyes and their eyes. The removers can be very harsh.

If you have been the technician to apply the lashes as per the instructions in this manual then the job should be easy.

First clean the clients face and eye area.

Then use a gentle toner to complete the cleaning process.

Cover the eye lid and the bottom lashes with tape and cotton pads.

Place a warm wet face cloth on the eyes for a few minutes.

Eyelash Extension Training

Soak a cotton ball with olive oil. Wipe it on the lashes, taking care not to get any in their eye. Continue gently wiping the lashes with oil until the extensions begin to fall off.

You may need to use a disposable mascara wand to assist with the breaking of the glue bond. I use two brushes one each side of the lashes and use a friction movement with the lashes between the brushes.

If the glue is thick and hard to remove you will need to use eyelash extension glue remover. However this is not advisable as it stings and damages the delicate skin on the eye lids.

Remove all the olive oil with a warm face cloth and then use a drop of toner on a cotton bud and clean the lashes.

I recommend having the client wash her face over your basin with a liquid cleanser and warm water to complete the cleaning process.

If you intend to clean her face and charge her be sure to rinse her face extremely well.

Dry her face.

Eyelash Extension Training

Have her get comfortable again on the bed.

Place a drop of olive oil on a cotton tip and smooth over the delicate eye skin close to but not on the lashes. Wait a few minutes and tap around the delicate eye area to bring more blood and oxygen to the skin surface. Then apply a warm wet face cloth. Next apply a cold pack.

Reapply cotton pads to beneath her bottom lashes and to her eyelid.

Place a small amount of glue remover to a disposable mascara wand. Remember I have said before glue remover is very hash and I try never ever to use it.

Try very hard not to get the glue remover on the skin. This is a complete work of art so put on your magnifying goggles.

With your pointy finger and your thumb, press down on the cotton pad so it will not move.

Eyelash Extension Training

With the wand in the other hand firmly and slowly brush down on the top lashes.

Then use the eyelash comb to comb the lashes. It will be a slow and tedious job. For this reason be sure to explain the cost to your client.

I recommend you write an eyelash removing leaflet and give to clients with a small kit.

The kit would contain:-
Four cotton pads
Three disposable wands
Two eye pads

They should attempt to remove the eyelashes them self at home with warm olive oil on a wand. If they are patient this is the best method.

They should put the olive oil in an oil burner or put oil on a one tablespoon and hold a match under the spoon to warm it. They can dip the wand in the oil.

Note some people say to heat the lashes as this softens the glue. Oh yes it will if you keep it going until the eyes almost burn. The glue sets like a rock after a day or so this is why less is best. You will never ever loosen the glue with heat. A warm cloth is to sooth the eyes not loosen or soften the glue. It will soften it the tiniest bit but not enough to remove the glue. Heat will only work if the lashes were glued on in the last hour or so. Extensions and false eyelash glue are two different molecular structures.

Structure and Shape Effects of Molecular Glue on Supramolecular Tubulin Assemblies

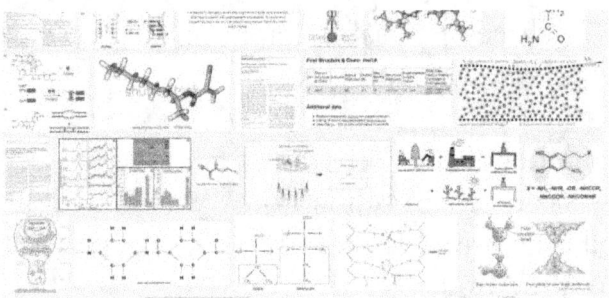

Is not a subject we even touch on in beauty training, is it now? If they did add it to beauty training they would have to add, at the very least another 150 hours to the course to even touch the surface of the types of bonds used in glue.

Eyelash Extension Training

Am I equipped to touch on this subject? Hell no. However I have used enough types of glue to know I hate them being used on our eyelashes. Can I recommend a great eyelash glue? No. After five decades of trying glues I am still not satisfied that a glue manufacturing company has even tried to produce a safe glue for us.

The only help I can give you is to warn you not to get it on the skin and to keep the glue 1 mm away from the lash root.

When I listen to the sales blubs at Beauty Expo I am greatly amused. I also think to myself. I have been there done that. I too have had blind, uneducated faith in what my suppliers tell me. The older we get the more we realize how little we know.

I like the video that this therapist has produced so watch her removing lashes.

http://www.wikihow.com/Remove-Eyelash-Extensions

I checked this video on the 30th July 2015 and it is still working. I do not like the written instructions on the page and you would be well advised to skip the process of reading them. Scroll down to the bottom of their page and watch the video.

My only constructive criticism is she did not apply a pad to the upper lid nor a protective layer of oil. No strips of tape to keep the eyes firm. These strips pull the eye skin taut and away from the lashes. They should be applied no matter how firm the clients skin is.

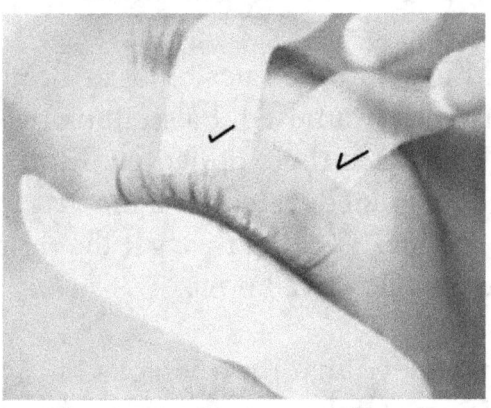

I dislike the use of petroleum jelly and baby oil which is a mineral oil. However in this case for eyelash removal they are a great product to protect the delicate eye area while removing lashes. Be very sparing and only give the eyes a tiny coat of one of these.

Eyelash Extension Training

This is a well trained therapist. After searching for three hours to find a video I could recommend to you, this therapist was the best I found. July 2010.

TEST 1 EYELASH EXTENSIONS

Eyelash Certificate Students only to do this test. However it will assist everyone wanting to apply lash extensions. The only difference is: - you will not have a teacher {like me} to debate the videos with.

Look up a few YouTube sites on eyelash extensions and email us the addresses to look at. Most movies go for 1-3 minutes. Your teacher will also look at the sites you have looked at and give you feed back on what they did right and wrong on the video you watched.

Take at least seven points from the ABOVE information and make an eye care sheet to give your clients. Send a copy to your teacher.

I have supplied one for you to view and the address of one video.

Understand this before you read my comments. When making videos the therapist is nervous. They also have to consider where the camera is so they are working in unnatural conditions. Under these circumstances they are doing a great job.

WATCH MOVIE CLIP ON GRAFTING

http://www.europeanbeautyconcept.com/

Copy and paste this site address into your web browser.
Click on Eyelashes
Click on educational movie.

This therapist opened three jars of lashes. Only open one at a time and put the lid back on straight away. Place the lashes on a sponge. Have a different sponge colour for each size lash. Then open the next jar with the next size lash, then the third jar with the next size lashes.

Place the pads with the lashes on, in sized order. Or buy them in strips but this is more expensive and sometimes they are very hard to get off the strip.

Eyelash Extension Training

Pots of lashes are the cheapest way to buy lashes. There is one size per pot. The most used sizes are 8 mm, 10 mm and 12 mm. The only issues I have found are there are sometimes some odd shaped lashes and some lashes are half a lash. You get a great number of lashes per jar, so that did not bother me.

This is a slightly slower method because you sprinkle the lashes on a pad and they are all sitting in different directions. You pick a lash up then you have to use the other set of tweezers to put the lash in the tweezers the way you need them to sit and then swop hands. That is time consuming.

As pictured below you can purchase them in strips. They come several ways. One strip

Eyelash Extension Training

can have all of one size or some strips can be purchased as a multi strip with about two rows of each different size.

When buying strips pay the extra money and buy them locally. They can often be moisture damaged and when they are damages from moisture they are a nightmare to work with. I purchased a large quantity from Beauty Expo once, off an Asian stand. Not one strip was usable. They were hard to remove from the strip and when I did manage to get a lash off the strip, each lash had paper attached to the end.

However if you can get fresh lashes from a reputable supplier they are the best to use.

Eyelash Extension Training

They are a perfect shape and thickness. They are easy and quick to use. But only when they are in an individual sealed box per strip.

It is best to buy them in one size per strip and have an application board that you apply the three sizes you need onto the board.

This therapist wiped the excess clue on the tape under the client's eyes. Never do that you can put an extra piece on tape on their cheek if you want. Also see my other suggestions below in the YouTude video.

http://www.youtube.com/watch?v=Z5LQimFojKI

In this video the therapist positions the lash with the tweezers that she applied the lash with. Never ever allow your tweezers to come in contact with the glue. This will cause lots of problems. The main problem will be the tweezers will glue together and with glue on the tweezers other natural lashes may stick to the tweezers. When she applies the second lash she uses the correct tool to position the lash. Never wipe the glue onto the clients eye pad. Have a small glass pad sitting near the client's neck or on her chest. I use a plastic

Eyelash Extension Training

wrap under the eye not these white pads. They pull too much on the sensitive skin around the eyes. They are fine if you cut them in half. She also puts the glue too close to the skin.

With that said, for your education purposes I would like to add, it is a nerve racking experience being on video while you are working. Unlike movie makers that have a big budget to produce a movie with lots of reruns these therapist get one shot.

HOW TO SUBMIT YOUR EXAMS

Only do this test if you are doing a full course with Beauty School Books.

Note: Here at Beauty School Books we are not an accredited beauty school and we only cater for students that are unable to attend a beauty school.

Email answers to or
mailto:beautyschoolbooks@gmail.com

Eyelash Extension Training

If you are training yourself you can request some video conference time with me for a small fee. Use Skype as the carrier.

If you have already been trained and you are reading this book to improve your skills you are to be congratulated.

If you are training at a beauty school you should feel very proud. There is no better way to train than to attend a quality school.

In the subject line put the course name and the test name.

In the body put your student header sheet with your personal details.

Then attach the test answers.

Your header sheet must contain;-

The test and course name
Your name
Date of Birth
Address
Telephone
Email address.

Eyelash Extension Training

FORMS FOR CLIENT

The first thing you need to understand is this is a training manual I cannot possible set it all out for you in the manual. Some people may need this manual delivered as an eBook. All eBook readers are different sizes so I am limited to formatting requirements. However I am happy to email forms to you. There is a small fee.

Please adjust to suit client having Eye Enhancement treatment. Then forward to your teacher for feedback.

Sample client treatment plan eye enhancement should contain:-

Name:
Address:
Tel. Work:
Tel. Home:
Occupation:
D.O.B.:
Medical conditions:
Lifestyle factors:

Here you need to know about their sporting activities. If they swim a lot, ask them to keep their head above water for a few days and explain they may need more infills than another client.

General health: Excellent, good, poor
Medication
Known allergies:
 Ask all the illness questions.
Do you have AIDS,
 Hepatitis,
 Heart Condition,
 Do you faint?
Have Diabetes,
Eye water a lot,
Conjunctivitis,
Have you taken any drugs today, when did you last have a drink of alcohol, have many glasses, of what,
Skin type:
Skin condition:
 Skin Type: Combination,
 Dry,
Oily,
 Dark,
 Fair,
Olive,
Youthful,
 Mature,
Dehydrated.

Eyelash Extension Training

Notes:
Previous treatments:
Contra-indications:
Comments / request
Treatment,
Therapist
Date
Price
30 lashes /25 lashes
Second layer yes /no

Set the form up like this below picture. The more professionally your forms are set out the easier it will be for you to fill them in. The client expects to be asked questions.

When you also ask appropriate questions they feel they are in the hands of a professional.

Make the form very quick and easy to fill in with lots of yes and no answers. That way it will be quick to fill in. If you have to write down all their answers it could take an hour.

Eyelash Extension Training

You can set this type of form pictured here in the program called Excel.

Name:			
Address:		Tel Work:	Tel Home:
Occupation:		D.O.B:	
Medical conditions:		Lifestyle factors:	
		Here you need to know about their sporting activities. If they swim a lot ask them to keep their head above water for a few days and explain they may need more infills than another client.	

General health:	Medication:	Known allergies:
☐ excellent ☐ good ☐ poor		

Skin type:	Skin condition:		Notes:
☐ normal	☐ blemished	☐ coupe rose	
☐ oily	☐ dehydrated	☐ prematurely aged	
☐ dry	☐ sensitive	☐ other	
☐ combination	☐ mature	☐ Eye water a lot	

Previous treatments:	
Body condition:	Postural condition:
Contra-indications:	
Comments / requests:	

TREATMENT	THERAPIST	DATE	PRICE
50 lashes / 25 lashes			

TEST TWO,

PRACTICE EYELASH EXTENSION.

Watch four YouTube videos.

Paste their address into a word document and write your comments on what you feel they did right and what you feel they did wrong.

Send to your teacher for her to watch and see if she agrees with your comments. If you do not have a personal trainer for this subject then at least you will have made the effort to improve your skills.

Then watch those movies again in a month time after you have studied and practiced some more.

Eyelash Extension Training

PRACTICE ON FALSE EYELASHES.

Practice on a set of false eyelashes. When you first start it is easier to attach the lashes to an orange or the dolls forehead.

Set up everything you need onto a tray.

TRAY SETUP FOR PRACTICE.

- The different size lashes,
- Glue,
- Glass or plastic square
- Tweezers 2-3 types
- Eyelash cleaner
- Eyelash blowers
- Eyelash curler
- Hand mirror
- Glad wrap or plastic wrap or eye tape
- Paper towel
- Headband
- An orange or a practice doll
- Q-Tips
- Eyelash brush and comb
- Tooth picks
- Orange stick

Eyelash Extension Training

- Cotton wool pads
- Gauge
- Tiny scissors
- Eye was bowl and solution

Place the lashes on a doll or an orange. Use a hobby glue to stick them down.

Now set up your work tray as though you are going to work on a client.

Read the instruction below for applying lashes.

Watch the DVD that came with your kit several times.

Remember the DVD is a video production so they have cut out mistakes the technician makes.

Now apply the grafted lashes to the false lashes.

Take a before, during and an after photo and send to your teacher.

Also take a photo of the amount of glue you are putting onto the lash.

Eyelash Extension Training

Add your Notes here as a reminder.

TEST THREE

EYELASH EXTENSION PRACTICE WITH TEACHER

You should have practiced at least five times before setting up an appointment with a teacher to watch you.

If you do not have a teacher you can book a web conference training session with Robyna. You will need Skype loaded onto your computer.

Email your details to
beautyschoolbooks@gmail.com

Send your telephone numbers and Robyna will call you if you live in Australia.

Internationals will need to correspond via email or Skype.

Set up a time with your teacher to watch you over video conference.

Eyelash Extension Training

You will need to have a relative or close friend willing to have the extensions done.

You will also need to have a friend to hold the camera near the eyes of the client you are working on.

If you do not have a teacher it is still a good idea to film yourself doing your lashes on the doll and on the live person.

Watch these videos so you can view your mistakes.

If the lashes are too long you can always trim them just a bit. Never trim too much or they will stick out.

Add your Notes here as a reminder.

Eyelash Extension Training

ADVERTISE YOUR SERVICE.

Flyers are a great way to advertise your business. Have one in your shop window and do a letter box drop.

Eyelash Extension Training

TEST FOUR

Now make up a flyer and put up on the window of your shop.

If you are a mobile therapist make smaller versions and put up on notice boards.

Be sure you add your business name and telephone number to the flyer.

I would add a set of made up eyes to this poster. You can buy photos on the internet or take a lovely photo of a client and ask her permission in writing to use the photo.

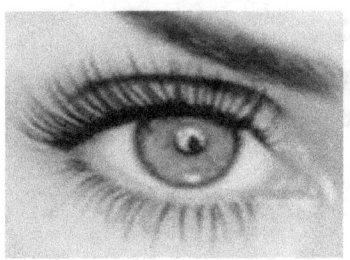

However this photo is after mascara has been added. It is best to have a photo of the completed lashes with and without mascara. This photo is before they have been dried and re brushed.

Eyelash Extension Training

AFTERCARE INSTRUCTIONS

Within the next 24 hours...

Try not to cry or go out into the wind. Water Eyes are salty and will dissolve the glue.

Avoid oil-based cleansers, lotion or eye makeup removers. These products will dissolve the eyelash bonding agent. Instead, use plain water or water-based gel cleansers or aromatherapy cleansers with a gel base.

You may wish to use a Q-tip to gently remove eye makeup around the lash line.

Do not use waterproof mascara. The ingredients in this type of mascara will dissolve the bonding agent and your lashes will fall off when you take the mascara off.

If you feel you must wear mascara... apply only" water-based" mascara on your lash tips, not at the base of your lashes. Application at the lash base may break the lash and/or create a clump of mascara in your lash line.

Eyelash Extension Training

Again, most women do not feel the need to apply any mascara at all. If you accidentally drop some powder on your lashes, simply remove with a Q-tip moistened in plain water in order for your dark lashes to reappear again.

Avoid using a mechanical eyelash curler. Instead, use a heated eyelash curler sparingly. Prolonged heat to the lashes may cause them to come loose as it will weaken the glues bond.

Schedule a "touch-up" procedure in 2-3 weeks. "Touch-ups" or "infill" are highly recommended in order to maintain a full, lush lash line. I swim every day and have to get my face under the shower with water pelting onto my face. I love the water. Therefore I need my infill done every two weeks.

Should the lashes become annoying then take them off and give lashes a break for a few weeks.

First apply a warm compress to the lashes to break the glue bond.

Eyelash Extension Training

Pat dry.

You can remove them by gently rubbing with olive oil.

Then apply a warm compress or book in to have the salon staff remove them for you.

You should have an infill done every two-three weeks.

TEST 5

Aftercare Instructions

Make up an aftercare sheet with your salon details and email to your teacher.

~~~ * ~~~

Eyelash Extension Training

PARTY LASHES

WHAT ARE PARTY LASHES?

Party lashes can be a row of lashes called "False Eyelashes" or Bunches of Lashes.

BUNCHES OF LASHES

Bunches of lashes know as party lashes.

Bunches of lashes are groups of lashes bonded together. You can just place a few at the outside edge of your natural lashes or place a full or half a row of them on your natural lashes. When glued 1 mm above the root of the natural lash onto the natural lash, they will last for two to four weeks.

Eyelash Extension Training

This will naturally depend on several conditions.

THE GLUE IRRITATION

The less glue that is used is the best. Too much glue will cause irritation to the eyes and cause the natural lashes to droop and become very heavy. The glue sets hard and becomes very prickly/sharp and will pierce the soft tissues around the eyes. This causes an uncomfortable situation and the person will want to constantly rub their eyes. When their lashes droop they can see a dark showdown and this will cause them to push the lashes up out of their line of sight.

When you dip the end of the lash in the glue, wipe off the excess on a piece of foil or a plastic dish.

The quality of the glue is vital. Never ever put glue into the refrigerator. Glue should be tossed into the bin after a few months and new glue purchased. You will know when it is time to dispose of the glue when it is hard to coat the end of the lash with the glue.

Eyelash Extension Training

When you attach a couple of lashes use a tooth pick to roll off the excess glue from the underside of the lashes. The toothpick should only be used once then a new one used on the next few lashes. I actually do this with every bunch I place onto the natural lash lashes.

FALSE LASHES

False lashes are usually a string of lashes. The type of glue used is designed for them to stay on for just a few hours. This service can be offered at the salon or you can sell them over the counter to customer. They come in a variety of thicknesses and shapes.

With all false, part and grafted lashes the glue and lashes should be glued to the natural lash not the skin.

Bunches of lashes and false lashes come in a multitude of lengths and styles.

Some have feathers on the outer edge and some have diamonds on the tips of the lashes. They can be flirty, natural looking or extreme.

Eyelash Extension Training

The reason we call them party lashes is because they are intended for a party. They will usually only stay on for a few hours to a few days. They are glued on the natural lashes close to the root of the natural lash.

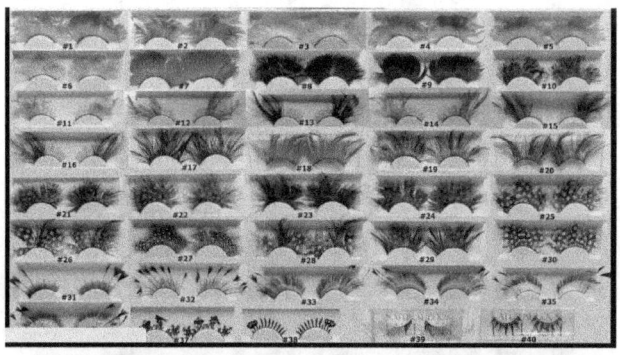

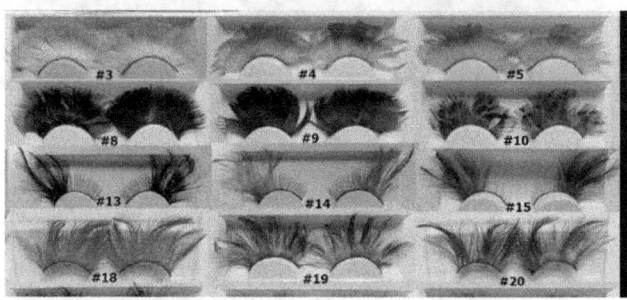

Eyelash Extension Training

Rows of false lashes

A variety of these is a must have in your kit. You hold one row on the clients eye, just one of her eyes.

This way both you and her can decide what type of lashes to apply.

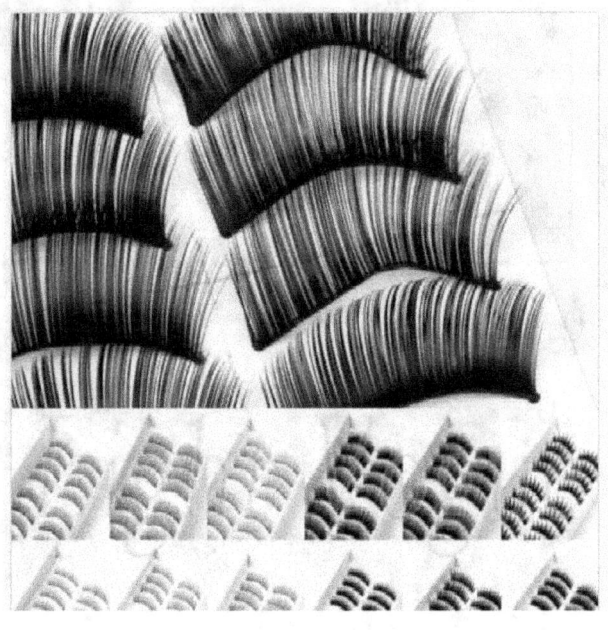

I have found eBay has an endless supply of party lashes. Type " False lashes" into their search engine {bar) and you will be pleasantly surprised.

EYELASH EDUCATION

People need to be informed on how to care for their lashes and cleaning of their face.

You need to have experienced both types of lashes using a few different glues before you can fully understand how to write up an education sheet for a client. The education sheet should be on the back of the aftercare sheet.

Party lashes are designed to last a few hours. However with the way we have applied them for you, you should be able to get a week or more from your lovely lashes. For Party lashes to last 1-3 weeks, it is best to wash your face with cold or cool water.

It is best not to dive into a swimming pool or the ocean. Just walk in and keep your head above water.

Best not to get the lashes wet for 12 hours after they have been attached.

Eyelash Extension Training

Best not to wear too much eye makeup that needs removing with oil based cleanser.

Try not to rub your eyes.

Try not to cry.

Try not to get your foundation or powder onto the lashes.

Do not apply mascara unless you are happy for them not to last.

Return to the salon before they are too thin. In other words if you are going somewhere on Saturday try to have an infill done on Thursday or Friday or best still on the Saturday. If we are applying party lashes or false eyelashes then it is best to have them applied just hours before the event. If your eyelashes still look great after two weeks make an appointment to have an infill in the beginning of the third week. For false eyelashes they should be removed and reapplied. I try never to go for four weeks before having my infill. That way my lashes always look great.

Eyelash Extension Training

These instructions apply to both party lashes and grafted lashes. However grafted lashes will definitely last longer than party lashes and have been designed that way.

Grafted lashes look more natural and will stay on longer because they are attached from near the root to the tip of each of your own personal lashes.

Here I would add a good close up shot of each type of lash service you offer in your salon.

~~~ * ~~~

Students by incorporating an education and an after care sheet to suit both types of lashes is the smart option.

It serves you in several ways.

1. *Less forms to worry about*
2. *You'll be less inclined to give out the wrong instruction sheet.*
3. *It lets the client know about both services.*

Eyelash Extension Training

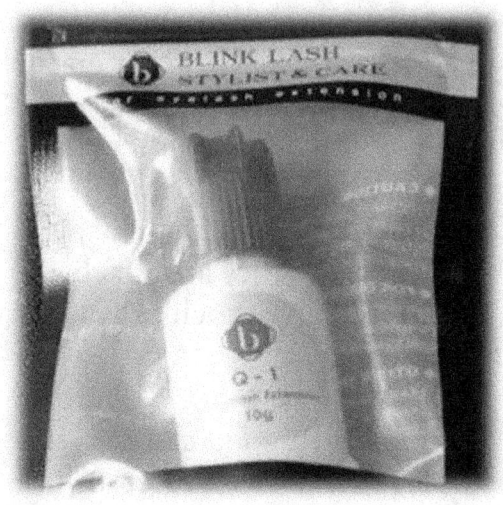

Blink Lash Style and care Glue. They say it is the best on the market today. No sting and dries quickly. Never ever keep any glue in the refrigerator.

The quality of the glue is vital. Never ever put glue into the refrigerator. Glue should be tossed into the bin after a few months and new glue purchased. You will know when it is time to dispose of the glue when it is hard to coat the end of the lash with the glue.

When you attach a couple of lashes use a tooth pick to roll off the excess glue from the underside of the lashes. The toothpick should only be used once then a new one used on the next few lashes. I actually do this with every bunch I place on the lashes.

APPLYING GLUE TO STRIP LASHES

First you have used tweezers to gently remove the lash from the pack.

Hold the lash to your eye and take a good look at the length and the shape.

Next trim the lash to suite your eyes length and shape.

Trim from the outer corner where the longer lashes are. Do not trim the inner corner or they will not graduate in shape and will look very artificial.

Do not apply too close to the inner corner or the lashes will feel like they are stabbing you during the day.

Do not curl the natural lashes as they say to do in some of the instructions that come

Eyelash Extension Training

with the eyelashes. This will make the placement of the false lashes almost impossible.

You do not want the lashes to extend all the way to the outer edge of your eye they will make you look tired.

For a mature aged person it is better that the lashes are longer in the middle. This will make the eyes more wide open.

The flick lash effect is for younger people.

Apply glue to a stick. This will save money on brushes and save cleanup time.

Then slide the lash along the stick you placed the glue on.

Eyelash Extension Training

Then slide the lash along the stick where there is no glue to smooth out the glue line and remove excess glue.

Sit the eyelash down on a dish for a minute or two so the glue sets a little before you apply. Be sure to sit them upside down so the glue does not touch the dish.

Look down into a magnifying mirror.

Then drop the lash onto your natural lashes.

Next wait a minute so the glue is almost dry. Then squeeze your natural lashes and the false lashes together. Start at the inner edge and work your way along the lashes.

Eyelash Extension Training

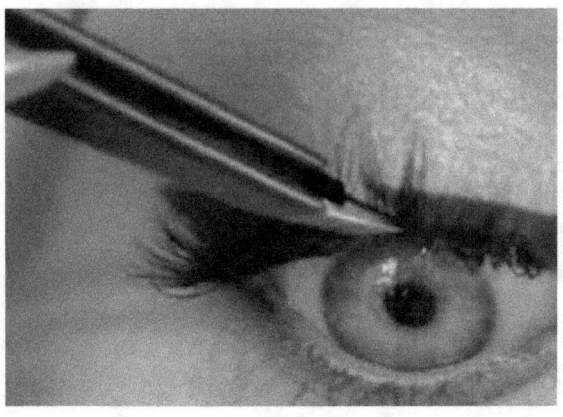

Use a light pressure you do not want to remove all the glue.

Use black glue not a clear, as clear glue turns whitish when dry.

When they are both in place, run a line of black eyeliner along the joint. Liquid eyeliner is best.

Next very gently run mascara under the natural lashes so blend the colour of the false lashes and your natural lashes.

Watch this video.
https://www.youtube.com/watch?v=-jigicP1Qvo

Eyelash Extension Training

The only thing I disagree with she adds the glue to the lashes. It is best to apply the glue to an orange stick or chop stick (must be a wooden one).

Then run the false lash along the stick and then run along the other end of the stick to remove the excess glue.

You will love her very bright bubbly personality. More to the point she gives an excellent tutorial. I watched twenty videos before choosing which one to recommend to you my faithful readers.

PARTY LASHES, VERSES GRAFTED LASHES.

Grafted lashes look very natural. They last for several weeks. Party lashes last from a few hours to a few days.

You can also add mascara and dive into a pool or the ocean when you have Grafted Lashes.

Grafted lashes take 1 hour to 2 hours to apply. Party lashes take 10 – 15 minutes to apply.

Grafted Lashes cost from $100 to $250 to have applied.

Party lashes cost $20 to $75 to have applied.

The glue for grafted lashes costs $76 the glue for Party lashes cost about $12. Both glues will be used for at least 6 sets of lashes.

Eyelash Extension Training

However both glues must be used within two months.

WATCH YOU TUBE VIDEO

Many years ago this was the best video I could find. Now days there are better ones to watch but it is well worth your time.

http://www.youtube.com/watch?v=e-acf94MOxk&feature=related

GRAFTED EYELASH KIT

4 Jars of Mink Lashes
1 Jar Eyelash Cleaner
Eyelash Brush
2 Sets of Tweezers
1 Air Pump to dry lashes
1 Jar of glue
1 Jar of eyelash remover.
1 Roll of tape to protect lower lashes
1 set of practice lashes
See our website for an updated Eyelash

Eyelash Extension Training

You will also need:-
- Cottonwool pads good quality.
- Cotton tips
- Paper towel
- Dental chain
- Beauty Bed
- 2 large towels. 1 goes under client 1 on top of client.
- 2 large hand towels. One goes around her feet. One around her neck secured with the dental chain
- 2 pillows. One goes under their shoulders and one under their knees.
- A good quality cleanser
- A good quality toner.

Buy a few more sets of tweezers as the ones in the kit do not suit everyone.

If you can afford a doll we recommend you buy one from a hairdressing supplier. It is great to have a doll on display with one eye done with party lashes and one with eyelash grating in your shop window. Add a sign to sit in front of the doll. It draws in business.

A TYPICAL EYELASH EXTENSION KIT

1st Allow me to explain the eyelashes come in jars with hundreds in each jar. Some come attached to a piece of cardboard.

They come in a "J" shape and a "C" shape "C" shape is the most popular so that is what we include in our kit

They come in 2-3 thicknesses

They come in several colours.

Usually Black, Brown, Blue, Purple, Green and Red,

Suppliers usually just send Black Lashes.

Eyelash Extension Training

LARGE KIT

A large Kit is not necessary for you to start off with. But this is what would come in a large kit.

- 3 Premium eyelash 0.15mm diameters, each 1 case (1gram) of 8 mm / 10 mm /12mm
- 3 Premium eyelash 0.20mm diameters, each 1 case (1gram) of 8mm / 10mm / 12mm
- 3 Premium coloured eyelash 0.15mm diameter, blue/purple/pink, each 1 case (1gram)
- Glue black 1 bottle (sensitive) 10ml,
- Glue black 1 bottle (very strong) 10ml,
- Glue Remover high grade 1 bottle 10ml,
- 1 Volume-up Mascara
- 3 Sets of tweezers curved type to select real lash for extension 3 pieces, Straight type to spread glue on lash. However I use an orange stick for this.
- Heated eyelash curler
- Mini handy mirror 1 pc,
- Good quality Irish diamond circle type for glue base

Eyelash Extension Training

- 2 Good quality rubber sponge to clean around eyes,
- Mini scissors for eyelash 1 pc,
- Handy type rubber air-blower 1 pc,
- False eyelashes for practice 1 pair,
- Medical adhesive tape for application work,
- Comb-brush for eyelash 1 pc,
- 1 Eyelash curler
- 1 Beauty Case 275mm(L) x 165mm(W) x 195mm(H)

Note: Unless you are going to be doing a lot of eyelash extensions this kit is too expensive. The glue does go off after about six month- one year. Buy a kit with only one bottle of glue.

If you do your work correctly there will be no sting to the eyes from the glue. The glue becomes a problem if you get it on the skin or in their eyes.

Place it too close to the skin at the lash root or if you use too much.

Eyelash Extension Training

SMALL KIT CONTAINS:-

- 1 Premium eyelash 0.15 mm diameter, each 1 case (1 gram) of 8 mm/10 mm /12 mm
- 1 Premium eyelash 0.20 mm diameter, each 1 case (1 gram) of 8 mm / 10 mm /12 mm
- 1 Glue black 1 bottle (sensitive) 10 ml,
- Glue Remover high grade 1 bottle.
- Tweezers Curved type to select real lash for extension 3 pieces, Straight type to pick up extension lash.
- Good quality rubber sponge to clean around eyes. You will need lots as these are single use.
- Mini scissors for eyelash 1 pc,
- Handy type rubber air-blower 1 pc,
- False eyelashes for practice 1 pair ,
- Medical adhesive tape for application work ,
- Comb-brush for eyelash 1 pc,
- Beauty Case 275 mm(L) x 165 mm(W) x 195 mm(H) 1 pc

Note: You usually find that the tweezers that come in the kit do not squeeze together well enough to do the picking up of the lash. You

Eyelash Extension Training

will need to try several types of tweezers until you get the set that suites you. Also they are not surgical steel and cannot be autoclaved. Therefore you need to add a little plastic wrap to the tips to prevent cross contamination.

I try to buy medical grade tweezers so they can be sterilized.

Eyelash Extension Training

CERTIFICATE COURSE

We only offer video sessions for the training. If you have a beauty therapist or school nearby you are best to do the training session with them. After you have worked through this eyelash training manual watched some YouTube site and practiced on orange and the false lashes you will not need much training.

If you would like do a certificate course

Contact:-

Beauty School Books

http://www.beautyschoolbookks.com

Email
mailto:beautyschoolbooks@gmail.com

Beauty School Books site will soon be loaded with how to pages on all:-

Beauty tips

Eyelash Extension Training

Beauty books
Body Piercing
Hair Styles
Dreadlocks
Fashion Tips And More
Forms for your business can be purchased.

ASSOCIATIONS

Thats Great
http://www.thatsgreat.co

They have not had enough volunteers to man the site and keep it up to date. I may become the Secretary and I am looking for volunteers to man the web pages with improved information.

Association of Professional Australia Aestheticians.
Telephone 07 5575 9364 |L:
info@apaa.com.au | www.apaa.com.au
P.O Box 96 Robina QLD 4226

I also am a member of APAA. They have been in business now for 57 years. They are doing something right. Their website is loaded with adverts and they are the ones that the Government asked to write the Australian Standards in 1992 and then they commissioned myself and many other therapists to assist with the setting up of the Australian standards.

Their joining fee is around $70 and yearly about $255. To become a member means you can use the initials APAA after your name on your business card and place a poster outside your Salon telling people you are a professional ruled by a code of ethics. But check with them on their prices.

On YouTube
I am placing a series of short to the point videos on YouTube this year.
They are very homemade. Videos are not my proficiency. But I am sure they will help the beginners.
Here are some to watch on my YouTube channel. The ones on piercing will naturally interest you the most.

Eyelash Extension Training

Piercing.

How to Hold Forceps Eyebrow

http://www.youtube.com/watch?v=gFzp9hSq8Cg&feature=related

Navel set up

http://www.youtube.com/watch?v=Gzbs9hG-Jnk

Labret / Munroe

http://www.youtube.com/watch?v=hqzJjsFahqE
http://www.youtube.com/watch?v=k-GcDYExsdg

Rollers out of hair

http://www.youtube.com/embed/srxSPiTzkc0

Roller in hair

http://www.youtube.com/embed/29S19y9AEwo

Hair wefts

http://www.youtube.com/watch?v=Dm0ioafxmqk

Cosmetic tattoo machine

http://www.youtube.com/watch?v=wkQXs0ZXS18

Pencil in Eye brows

http://www.youtube.com/watch?v=8pN5o7BADbU

OTHER BOOKS BY THIS AUTHOR

In 1995 I started writing training manuals for other companies. Prior to that, I had a protocol book in each of my salons for the staff. On each procedure I had a page for the room setup, client comfort, Tray setup procedures and Procedure step by step instructions. I have now added those note to what I call my "Beauty School Books Training manuals" I always said one day I would write books for the industry and here they are:-

HEALING AND TRAINING MANUALS

DOG CARE & DIY ORGANIC MEDICATIONS

Take care of your pets with aromatherapy cures. Make your own flea treatments shampoos and many healing products organically within seconds for your pets.

FOOLPROOF AROMATHERAPY

Essential oils can heal, sooth and energise. Learn how to mix. When not to use and all the benefits for hundreds of ailments listed in alphabetical order. User friendly.

THE ANTIQUE HEALER

This is a much large Aromatherapy book with photos and more healings. Also contains wise old women's remedies.

I WAS NOT READY TO LOSE MY MOTHER

My mother had a few weeks to live. Her Cancer was very aggressive. I set her up on a healing program of juices, essential oils and herbs. This was all working until she stopped the program. It also has a lovely storey about her life. Married at age 16 until her Passover at 83 years of age.

BODY PIERCING BASICS

All the main points on body piercing.

ANATOMY FOR BODY PIERCERS

All Body Piercers should understand the body and how it works this is a wonderful tool for any Body Piercer.

EYELASH EXTENSION GRAFTED LASHES TRAINING MANUAL

Step by step instructions with video tutorials. Which you are reading now.

Eyelash Extension Training

EYEBROW SHAPING AND TINTING TO SUIT FACE SHAPES

Step by step instructions with video tutorials on eyebrow shaping, eyelash and brow tinting.

COSMETIC TATTOO PERMANENT MAKEUP MICRO-PIGMENTATION TRAINING MANUAL

A step by step training manual. You could actually teach yourself the trade as this book is so well written.

AN ANGEL FOR COSMETIC TATTOOISTS

A helping hand for a cosmetic tattooist.

HAIR EXTENSIONS TRAINING MANUAL

Learn to create hair wefts, weaves, braids, wax in, and clip in Hair Extensions. There are videos to watch in the eBook.

SUPERNATURAL BOOKS:-

SPELL FOLKLORE

A great book on how to do some positive affirmations also called spells.

TAROT SCROLLS 0-22

Eyelash Extension Training

Ask a question open a page and an inspiring answer will be there for you to read.

CHILDREN'S BOOKS:-

ROMEO AND JULIETTE KEEP MARK ANTONY

A wonderful storey about a puppy born on a boat. His white cute and fluffy. True storey with a dash of magic added.

MARK ANTONY MARRIES LIZY AND HAS PUPPIES

Loaded with photos of all the dogs and the new born puppies. A true story with a dash of fantasy added.

~~~~ *** ~~~~

This Author releases a book every year. Contact Robyna at :-

mailto:beautyschoolbooks@gmail.com

Also keep an eye on her face book page.

http://www.facebook.com/robynasmithkeys

Eyelash Extension Training

Good luck everyone I pray this manual will assist you to flutter up with great looking lashes. I am only ever an email away from you if you are cross examining yourself or any information you have read.

It is hard to give you everything I think you need to know to become a great Beauty Therapist. Each of my Beauty School Books has its main topic and the title of each book contains hopefully all you need to know about that subject. I often add extracts from some of my other books as it seems relevant at the time of written for you.

I would like to take this opportunity to tell you how smart you are. Anyone that takes time to read all they can find on any given subject is a blessing to our trade. You are a play safe individual.

Congratulations

From Roby x

~~~ *** ~~~

Eyelash Extension Training

Milliliters	Ounces (U.S.)	Ounces (U.K.)
1.00	0.03	0.04
10.00	0.34	0.35
20.00	0.68	0.70
30.00	1.01	1.06
40.00	1.35	1.41
50.00	1.69	1.76
60.00	2.03	2.11
70.00	2.37	2.46
80.00	2.71	2.82
90.00	3.04	3.17
100.00	3.38	3.52

www.ingramcontent.com/pod-product-compliance
Lightning Source LLC
Chambersburg PA
CBHW051526230426
43668CB00012B/1753